All About Roses

Created and designed by
the editorial staff of
ORTHO BOOKS

Writers
Rex Wolfe
James McNair

Illustrator
Ron Hildebrand

Designer
Gary Hespenheide

Ortho Books

Publisher
Robert B. Loperena

Editorial Director
Christine Jordan

Manufacturing Director
Ernie S. Tasaki

Managing Editor
Sally W. Smith

Editor
Robert J. Beckstrom

Prepress Supervisor
Linda M. Bouchard

Editorial Assistants
Joni Christiansen
Sally J. French

Address all inquiries to:
Ortho Books
Box 5006
San Ramon, CA 94583-0906

Copyright © 1983, 1990, 1995
Monsanto Company
All rights reserved under international and Pan-American copyright conventions.

3	4	5	6	7	8	9
	97	98	99	2000		

ISBN 0-89721-256-8
Library of Congress Catalog Card Number 94-69601

THE SOLARIS GROUP
2527 Camino Ramon
San Ramon, CA 94583-0906

Acknowledgments

Photography Editor
Judy Mason

Editorial Coordinator
Cass Dempsey

Copyeditor
Toni Murray

Proofreader
David Sweet

Indexer
Trisha Lamb Feuerstein

Layout by
Indigo Design & Imaging

Separations by
Color Tech Corp.

Lithographed in the USA by
Banta Company

Special Thanks to
Paula and Donald Ballin
Chicago, Ill.

Tom Bressan, Urban Farmer
San Francisco, Calif.

Thomas Cairns
Los Angeles, Calif.

Tom Carruth, Weeks Roses
Upland, Calif.

David Van Ness
El Cerrito, Calif.

Jim West, Soil and Plant Laboratory
Santa Clara, Calif.

Front Cover
'Mon Cheri', an All-American Rose Selection winner for 1982, is graced by a spicy fragrance, as well as a two-toned bloom.

Title Page
Floribunda 'Marina'

Back Cover
Top left: *Rosa wichuraiana*, the Memorial Rose. This old species rose is still popular in modern gardens.
Top right: Climbing rose 'Don Juan' is a natural for covering a fence.
Bottom left: Floribunda rose 'Intrigue', an All-America Rose Selection.
Bottom right: 'Duet' was grafted to a strong trunk to make this tree form.

The Board of Directors of the American Rose Society authorized me to enthusiastically endorse the book *All About Roses*. This book is one of the best and most complete of its kind being sold in the United States today. In my opinion this book should enable you, the reader, to grow and enjoy roses as they are meant to be enjoyed.

Pete Haring

Pete Haring
President, 1994–1997
The American Rose Society

Photographers
Names of photographers are followed by the page numbers on which their work appears.
R = right, C = center, L = left, T = top, B = bottom.

Martha Baker: 8TL, 18, 94BL, 95BC, 96BR
Cathy Wilkinson Barash: 99BC
Laurie A. Black: 39, 43, 56, 86L
Thomas Cairns: 101BR
Derek Fell: 9B, 32
Barbara J. Ferguson: 81BL, 91L, 91TR, 93TR
John Frost: 97TR
Linda Garcia: 29T, 88TR
P. A. Haring: 12T, 26T, 26B, 29B, 74TL, 74BL, 74BR, 76BL, 76BR, 77TR, 77BR, 78L, 78TR, 78BR, 79L, 79TC, 79TR, 79BC, 80TL, 80R, 81TL, 82TC, 82TR, 82BL, 83BL, 86BR, 87TR, 87BR, 90BL, 95BR, 96TL, 96TR, 98L, 99TR, 100BR, 101TL, 101BL, 102, 105, 107, back cover BL
Saxon Holt: 16, 103B, back cover BR
Muriel Humenick: 75BL
Jackson and Perkins: 60, 61
Kathryn Kleinman: 66, 67
Susan M. Lammers: 90TL
Michael Lamotte: 20B, 64, 68, 69
Burton Litwin: 100TR, 101TR
Robert Lowe: 75BR
Michael McKinley: 10, 25, 28, 73R, 76TL
James McNair: 20TC, 82TL
Ortho Information Services: 20TR, 21, 36, 49, 88BR, 95BL
Photo/NATS: Cathy Wilkinson Barash—22, 84BR, 95T
Photo/NATS: Gay Bumgarner—94BR
Photo/NATS: Priscilla Connell—75TL, 81BR, 86TR, 99L
Photo/NATS: John A. Lynch—74TR
Photo/NATS: A. Peter Margosian—87L
Photo/NATS: Ann Reilly—front cover, 4, 14, 81TR, 82BR, 83R, 84TL, 84BL, 85BL, 88L, 89L, 96BC, 99TC, 104T
Ann Reilly: 1, 7, 8TR, 8B, 9TL, 9TR, 12B, 13, 15, 20TL, 30, 33, 34, 44, 48, 70, 72TR, 72BR, 73BL, 75TR, 76TR, 77L, 80BL, 83TL, 84TR, 84BC, 85TL, 85TR, 85BR, 89TR, 89BR, 90R, 91BR, 92L, 92TR, 92BR, 93TL, 93TC, 93BL, 93BR, 94TL, 96BL, 97BR, 98R, 99BR, 100L, 103T, 104C, 104B, 106, back cover TL
Susan A. Roth: 17, 72L, 73TL, 97L, back cover TR
Joe Schopplein: 6L, 6R
J. J. Scoville: 79BR
George Taloumis: 24

All About Roses

The History and Development of the Rose

Roses have been cultivated for centuries in many lands. Today's gardener can choose from a wide selection, from old favorites to new examples of the hybridizer's art.

The rose is often proclaimed "queen of the flowers" by gardeners, and there are few flowers that can make a better claim to the title. Roses are grown primarily for the beauty and fragrance of their flowers, which can be found in an astonishing array of shapes and sizes and in almost every color of the spectrum. Roses have been tended and enjoyed by generations of modern-day gardeners, and their lineage under cultivation stretches back many hundreds of years.

Species of the genus *Rosa* have been identified almost everywhere in the Northern Hemisphere, as far north as Alaska and Norway and as far south as North Africa and Mexico. Fossilized plants over thirty million years old have been linked to modern rose species.

The Chinese were probably the first to cultivate roses. Five hundred years before the birth of Christ, Confucius wrote of the roses in the Imperial Gardens. Roses had been under cultivation in China for over two thousand years before China roses were introduced to the European market in the mid-eighteenth century.

Floribunda 'First Edition' bears a profusion of slightly fragrant, luminous blossoms.

Two illustrations from Redouté's 1824 masterpiece, Les Roses, provide a glimpse of early rose varieties. The work features 167 color plates of roses from all over the world dating from the classical period, the Middle Ages, and the early nineteenth century.

The seedbed of European rose growing was in the Middle East, in Persia and Mesopotamia, but little is known about the types of roses grown in those countries or the methods of cultivation. The ancient Persians established a flourishing trade in precious attar of roses, a fragrant oil distilled from rose petals, so they must have been adept at rose cultivation.

The ancient Greeks cultivated roses extensively—for the beauty of the flowers, for medicinal purposes, and for perfume. They dedicated the rose to two deities: Aphrodite, the goddess of love and beauty, and Dionysus, the god of revelry. They fashioned wreaths and garlands of roses for festivals in honor of the gods.

It was during the height of the Roman Empire (the first three centuries after the birth of Christ) that rose cultivation reached its peak in the ancient world. The Romans imported roses from Egypt and established a thriving rose-growing industry at Paestum, south of Rome. They learned to force roses into bloom during winter by growing them in greenhouses or by irrigating them with warm water. Private rose gardens were universal among the rich and noble, and large public rose gardens were frequented and enjoyed by the populace.

The poet Horace half-jokingly expressed concern that the amount of land devoted to roses might cause a shortage of grain. Typically excessive, the emperor Nero spent vast sums of money to shower his guests with rose petals that he arranged to have fall from the ceiling. During the first century A.D., Pliny the Elder described several different species of roses in his *Natural History.*

After the fall of the Roman Empire and the demise of Roman culture, the rose fell into disfavor and was grown mostly in monastery gardens for its medicinal value: Roses were thought to be effective for a wide variety of ailments. The decorative qualities of roses could not remain ignored for long, however. After A.D. 1000 the plants began to appear in the manor gardens of the nobility. During the twelfth and thirteenth centuries, warriors returning from the Crusades in the Middle East brought back tales of splendid rose gardens and a few sample plants. Interest in and cultivation of roses began anew in Europe.

The 30 years of civil war in England during the fifteenth century, which became known as the War of the Roses, was not named thus because it was fought over roses; rather, it got its name from the two families fighting over the throne of England, the House of York and the House of Lancaster, who took the white rose and the red rose, respectively, as their emblems. Henry VII united the two families by marriage and created the Tudor rose, a white rose superimposed on a red, which is still the emblem of English royalty.

With the flowering of the Renaissance and its emphasis on beauty and design, roses again found favor in both private and public gardens. The expansion of commerce that was part of this period moved different varieties of roses throughout Europe and later to colonial outposts in the New World.

Two important sets of circumstances in the late eighteenth century led to the explosion in the popularity of roses that continues unabated to this day. The first was the introduction to the West of roses from China in 1752. Just about every modern rose can trace its ancestry to one of the roses imported from China. The second boost to the popularity of roses was given by the empress Josephine of France. After she married Napoleon in 1796, she set about creating at the Chateau Malmaison on the outskirts of Paris a garden that would contain exotic plants from all over the world. She became particularly intrigued with roses and set out to collect all the known varieties. Competition was fierce among the rose growers of the Continent and England; her patronage gave special impetus to the French breeders, who dominated the market until well into the twentieth century.

At the time of the empress's death in 1814, her garden at Malmaison contained over two hundred and fifty varieties, and collecting and growing roses had become a popular pastime for the fashionable set and the new merchant class alike. A further legacy of the empress Josephine was the encouragement she gave her drawing master, Pierre Joseph Redouté, to take up botanical illustration.

Redouté showed great talent in his exquisitely rendered watercolors, particularly in his 1824 masterpiece, *Les Roses*. Few illustrators since have approached his ability to render anatomical details accurately while at the same time capturing the beauty of the rose's color and form in an almost magical way.

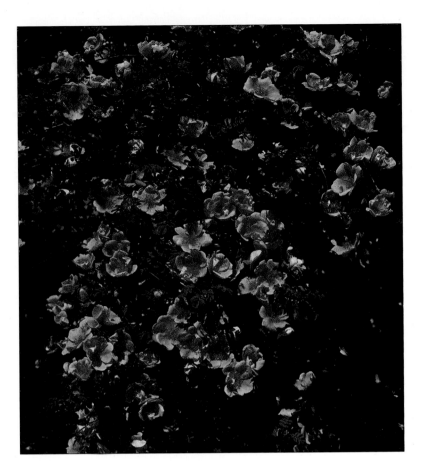

SPECIES, HYBRIDS, AND SPORTS

In the genus *Rosa* there are over one hundred and fifty types of roses that have specific characteristics. These species roses are plants that grow in the wild and from which all other roses are descended. Two different roses can cross-pollinate very easily to produce a rose that has some of the characteristics of each parent but an identity of its own. In this process, known as hybridization, pollen from one plant fertilizes the ovary of another. Plants grown from the resulting seeds are hybrids. Hybridization frequently happens in nature, with bees and other insects carrying the pollen, but modern hybridizers have developed the process to an intricate art. Because of their efforts, there are now thousands of different kinds of roses. The different plants within a species are called varieties. The varieties developed by hybridizers are called cultivars. (See pages 19 and 20 for a discussion of modern rose hybridizers and pages 59 to 61 for instructions on cross-pollination.)

Varieties and cultivars may be the result of a sport rather than hybridization. A sport is chance genetic mutation that occurs in a

Because of its distinct characteristics, Rosa hugonis (Father Hugo rose) was classified as a species rose when it was discovered in China in 1899.

Breeders produce exquisite colors through hybridization. The bicolored hybrid tea 'Double Delight' (right) is the dramatic result of crossing 'Granada' (top left) and 'Garden Party' (top right).

species or a hybrid. Sports resemble the other plants of their type but often have radically different flowers or growth habits. Roses sport in four different ways: change in the petal number, usually from single to double petals; change in the petal color; development of moss on the flower stems and sepals; and change from a bush to a climbing habit.

CLASSIFICATION OF ROSES

With so many roses to choose from, gardeners need some sort of classification system. Roses are divided into three broad types: species roses, old garden roses, and modern roses.

Species roses, as discussed previously, are those found growing in the wild. Old garden roses, often simply called old roses, are those

'Chicago Peace' (left), a sport of the hybrid tea 'Peace' (right), is the charming result of a chance genetic mutation.

varieties and cultivars that can be clearly identified with a specific group of roses grown before 1867. This date was set by the American Rose Society to commemorate the introduction of what was considered to be the first hybrid tea rose, 'La France', during that year. All rose groups introduced after 1867 are classified as modern roses.

Species Roses

There are probably over one hundred and fifty species of roses in the world, although the exact number is disputable. Roses cross-pollinate so freely that it is difficult to determine whether a wild rose is a natural hybrid or a new species. True, unadulterated species plants are difficult to find because most have been improved on by rose breeders.

Some species roses bloom only once, during the spring or summer, but many have a second, lesser bloom in the fall. They usually have single flowers—that is, a single set of five petals—which have a simple and delicate appearance that many gardeners appreciate. Many species roses produce a decorative bonus of colorful and distinctive hips, or seedpods, in the fall.

Be sure to allow enough room for species roses, for some can grow 8 feet tall and as wide. Use them as a hedge, as specimen plants, or as

a magnificent backdrop for other plants. They require relatively little maintenance; for example, they require less pruning than modern roses. Most are hardy in cold climates, easily surviving without winter protection.

The following list briefly describes some species roses that can be grown successfully in gardens.

The introduction in 1867 of the first hybrid tea rose, 'La France', marked the beginning of the modern rose era. There are now thousands of modern roses.

Rosa banksiae   The Lady Banks' rose is a handsome evergreen plant that blooms once early in the season, producing great clusters of small double white or yellow flowers. Used on arbors, fences, and other structures, this vigorous rose climbs 20 feet or more. It is hardy and resistant to pests and diseases.

Rosa eglanteria   Plant this shrub, commonly called sweet briar rose or eglantine, in an upwind corner of the garden, someplace out of the way. It will quickly become a thick mass of canes that is difficult to control, but on moist and warm summer evenings the distinctively scented foliage will prove a delight. The small single pink flowers bloom for only a short period of time.

Rosa foetida   This rose is a spindly bush, not terribly vigorous, and needs a stake or a wall to grow against. It grows to 5 or 6 feet tall and 4 feet wide. The single flowers are brilliant yellow, with a heavy, unusual fragrance that is offensive to some people. It smells like clean linseed oil. *R. foetida* is best known for two sports: *R. foetida bicolor,* known as Austrian copper rose, which has petals that are orange-red on the face but yellow on the underside; and *R. foetida persiana,* known as the Persian yellow rose, which has luxuriant double yellow flowers. Both are very susceptible to blackspot, unfortunately, and should not be planted close to other roses in the garden.

Rosa glauca   This exceptional rose, also known as *R. rubrifolia*, is grown mainly for the decorative quality of its reddish brown bark and gray-green, slightly iridescent foliage. It grows to 6 feet tall and as wide, with an open habit. The small pink flowers bloom in the early summer.

Rosa hugonis   Commonly called the Father Hugo rose, this species was found by Father Hugh Scallon in China in 1899. It bears light yellow semidouble flowers with a slight yeasty fragrance on drooping branches. It grows 6 to 8 feet tall and almost as wide.

Rosa laevigata   Known as the Cherokee rose, this climbing species produces single, fragrant 3-inch blossoms that are creamy

Two forms of Rosa foetida *have been planted as a screen: the double-petaled Persian yellow rose (right) and the bicolored Austrian copper rose (left).*

white with contrasting gold stamens. This plant is not hardy in the far North.

Rosa moyesii   This vigorous species can grow as large as 12 feet tall and 10 feet wide. It has an open habit, however, so plants that like partial shade can be grown around it. Flowering begins in late spring and continues for several weeks. The 3-inch single flowers are blood red, with little scent. A popular hybrid offspring is 'Nevada', which has 3½-inch semidouble white flowers that bloom in amazing profusion in early summer and then repeat sporadically throughout the summer and fall.

Rosa rugosa   This very hardy species, known as the Japanese, ramanas, or rugosa rose, grows 3 to 6 feet tall and 4 feet wide. Fragrant single carmine-mauve flowers bloom from spring to fall, followed by large brilliant orange-red hips rich in vitamin C. The crinkled leaves are a shiny dark green. There are many fine forms, with flowers in varying shades of pink, white, and red. Rugosas will grow in almost any soil and are particularly recommended near the seashore. This plant can be trained into a good hedge.

Rosa spinosissima   This species, called the Scotch or burnet rose, is low-growing (around 3 feet) and spreads rapidly by means of suckers, making it a good ground cover. The single cream-colored flowers are fragrant. Forms with white, yellow, pink, or purple flowers are also available. Distinctive, almost black hips adorn the plant in fall.

Wilhelm Kordes, a famous German rose breeder, used *R. spinosissima* to create a spectacular succession of cultivars called the Frühlings series. 'Frühlingsgold' has huge semidouble golden yellow flowers 3½ to 5 inches across. Mature plants are much larger than *R. spinosissima*, growing 6 to 8 feet tall and almost as wide.

Rosa virginiana   A native of North America, this large (6 feet tall and 5 feet wide) shrub bears single pink flowers on long, arching canes in midsummer. It suckers vigorously, so confine it to a bed and keep the suckers cut back unless you want it to spread. 'Plena', with its double pink flowers and a slightly more compact habit, is a favorite hybrid.

Rosa wichuraiana   Known as the memorial rose, this native of East Asia is a low-growing, spreading plant ideal as a ground cover on a slope, since the stems root where they touch the ground. Slightly fragrant clusters of single and semidouble white flowers bloom in summer above lush green foliage.

Old Garden Roses

During the first half of this century, old garden roses were out of favor with the rose-buying public; in the spotlight were hybrid tea roses and other groups developed within the last hundred years or so. Recently there has been renewed interest in these old-fashioned roses, and a greater number of cultivars are becoming commercially available. This renaissance may stem from a nostalgia for the past. It may have come about because more gardeners want the powerful fragrance, disease resistance, and hardiness that many old roses possess, or simply because they enjoy the different flower forms of these roses. Whatever the case, rose fanciers welcome the increased availability of these remarkable flowers.

As mentioned previously, old roses are those groups of varieties and cultivars that were introduced before 1867, when the first hybrid tea rose, 'La France', appeared. However, new varieties in the old groups have been introduced since that time, and they, too, are classified as old roses. The following list describes the major groups of old roses in roughly the order that they were introduced.

Gallica   Records show that the French rose (*R. gallica*) was under cultivation in the sixteenth century, which makes it the earliest European species still in existence. The apothecary's rose (*R. gallica officinalis*) was grown during the Middle Ages in almost every monastery garden for use in a variety of herbal remedies.

Gallicas form compact bushes 3 to 4 feet high. Be careful if a gallica is growing on its own roots (that is, if it has not been grafted); it will spread quickly by runners unless it is kept under control. The fragrant flowers bloom once in early summer. They may be single, semidouble, or double, in shades of deep red through purple to pink; some varieties are marbled or striped with white. Gallicas are quite hardy and will tolerate poor soil.

Right: Apothecary's rose was first grown in the sixteenth century.
Bottom: 'Harison's Yellow' was spread across North America by settlers in the nineteenth century.

Damask The ancestors of damask roses were native to the eastern Mediterranean and were probably introduced to western Europe by Crusaders returning from the wars. The plants are 3 to 7 feet tall and are hardy, but they require good soil. They can be rangy; the arching canes may need to be staked so that the blossoms can be fully appreciated. The summer damask (*R. damascena*) blooms once in midsummer; the autumn damask (*R. damascena semperflorens*) usually has a second bloom in the fall. The medium-sized double or semidouble flowers in shades of pink to white grow in large clusters. Damask roses are particularly valued for their fragrance.

Alba The white rose of York (*R. alba*) is of uncertain parentage, but it was probably the white rose grown by the Romans, who introduced it as far north as England. It became very popular during the Renaissance, and it is often seen in Italian paintings of the period. Albas grow densely 6 to 9 feet tall with distinctive gray-green or blue-green foliage, and they are quite hardy and resistant to pests and diseases. They bloom once in late spring or early summer. The flowers are of medium size, usually semidouble, delicate, and fragrant, in shades of pink as well as white.

Centifolia These roses are derived from *R. centifolia* (literally, "hundred-leaved"), which has huge, very fragrant flowers and is known to many gardeners as the cabbage rose. Of uncertain parentage, it was first produced by Dutch hybridizers in the sixteenth century. Ranging in height from 3½ to 7 feet, centifolia roses have long canes that need staking or other support if the flowers are to be properly appreciated. The double blossoms appear in clusters once a year in late spring or early summer. They range in color from shades of reddish purple to pink, often with darker centers. Most centifolias are quite susceptible to powdery mildew.

Moss Close relatives of centifolias, moss roses made their debut in the late seventeenth century. They are similar to centifolias in growth habit and flowers, but their primary characteristic is a green or reddish brown mossy covering on the flower stems and sepals that is fragrant and sticky to the touch. Available in shades of white, pink, crimson, or reddish purple, most moss roses bloom only once, in early summer. They are quite hardy.

China The introduction to the West in 1752 of the first China rose (*R. chinensis*) was a milestone in the history of rose breeding. The China roses were *remontant*, or repeat blooming, flowering in early summer and again in the fall—a great improvement over most of the Western roses, which with the exception of the autumn damask have only one, relatively short blooming period a year.

Most Chinas are medium-sized plants with an open growth habit, good-looking as bedding plants or in containers. They are tender plants and prefer a moist soil. The flowers are small; they grow in clusters of pink, red, and crimson, with little fragrance.

Breeders were not immediately successful in producing crosses between the China rose and European species. In fact, the first cross was a natural one discovered on the Ile de Bourbon (now Reunion Island) in the Indian Ocean. 'Old Blush' cross-pollinated with an autumn damask rose, producing what came to be known as Bourbon roses.

Bourbon Among the most popular roses in the early nineteenth century, Bourbon roses

differ from their predecessors in that they produce blooms on new wood grown the same season. The flowers are semidouble or double, in shades of white, pink, red, and purple, with a slight apple scent. Their main blooming period is in midsummer, but most bloom again in the fall. The plants are vigorous, sometimes reaching 6 feet tall, and often need support. They are generally tender.

Portland These roses resulted from a cross between another China rose, 'Slater's Crimson China', and the autumn damask. These cultivars are similar to the Bourbon roses, but they have stronger colors and generally smaller flowers. They never achieved the great popularity of the Bourbons.

Tea Another import from China, the tea rose (*Rosa × odorata*) was introduced in the West in 1808. Closely related to China roses, these roses are distinguished by their distinctive tea fragrance and their larger, fuller flowers. The teas bloom through the summer into the fall, bearing semidouble or double blossoms in shades of white, pink, or yellow. Unfortunately, tea roses are quite tender.

Creamy yellow 'Frühlingsgold', a hybrid of a species rose, is considered an old garden rose even though it was developed during this century.

Noisette   The first hybrid rose group to originate in North America was the noisette, in 1818. Developed from a cross between the China rose and the musk rose (*R. moschata*), noisettes are climbers, growing up to 20 feet. Clusters of white, pink, yellow, or red flowers with a fragrance like that of the tea rose appear throughout the summer and fall. Noisettes are not hardy in the North.

Hybrid perpetual   This group is the precursor of the modern roses. It is impossible to determine exactly the parentage of these roses; they probably resulted from repeated crossings of noisettes, teas, Portlands, and Bourbons. Hybrid perpetuals became immensely popular during the last half of the 1800s, when over four thousand varieties were introduced.

Their popularity was well deserved. Hybrid perpetuals are hardy, vigorous plants that produce large (up to 7 inches), mostly double flowers. "Perpetual," however, is a bit of an overstatement: They bloom profusely in spring or early summer, rest a few weeks or bloom intermittently in summer, then usually bloom once more in the fall. The quality and quantity of the fall flowers vary from year to year. The fragrant blooms are usually solid colors ranging from white to pink to maroon.

Hybrids of species   This group consists of hybridized varieties of species roses such as *R. bracteata, R. sempervirens,* and *R. spinosissima.* 'Harison's Yellow', a hybrid of *R. foetida,* was developed in New York in the early nineteenth century and was spread across North America by settlers. A 5-foot shrub, it bears fragrant, bright yellow semidouble flowers in spring.

Modern Roses

The new groups of roses introduced after 1867 are classified as modern roses. Nearly all the roses found in local nurseries and garden centers are modern roses, as are those offered by most mail-order companies.

Plant breeders' sophisticated techniques have produced a great number of hybridized modern roses in a stunning array of colors, flower forms, numbers of blooms, and growth habits. There is a modern rose to delight every gardener. The main groups of modern roses are

hybrid teas, polyanthas, floribundas, grandifloras, miniatures, and shrubs.

Hybrid tea   Hybrid tea roses are the most widely grown roses in the world today. Long, narrow buds open into delicate blossoms on straight, tensile stems. Modern hybrid teas resulted from many decades of breeding and interbreeding between hybrid perpetuals and tea roses; they have gained hardiness and vigor from the former, and fragrance and delicacy of form from the latter.

In 1900 the breeder Joseph Pernet-Ducher introduced 'Soleil d'Or', a second-generation offspring of the Persian yellow rose (*R. foetida persiana*) and a hybrid perpetual. This was the first yellow hybrid tea, and its introduction opened up a whole new range of colors for hybridizers. For a number of years,

'Félicité et Perpétué', a climbing rose bred in France in 1827, is a hybrid of Rosa sempervirens.

*Pure white floribunda
'Class Act' is a 1989
All-America Rose
Selection.*

these brightly colored roses were known as Pernetianas, but they had been absorbed into the hybrid tea class by the 1930s.

Hybrid teas bloom prolifically from spring or early summer until the first frost; the blooming occurs in waves, with a short rest period between each wave. The flowers are borne singly on long stems. Usually double and often fragrant, they range in color from whites through lavenders, pinks, yellows, oranges, and reds, with mixtures and blends.

Generally, hybrid teas can survive winters without protection in areas where the average minimum winter temperature does not fall below 10° F. Bushes usually grow to 4 or 5 feet tall, although they may be smaller in cold-winter climates and taller in warm-winter areas. Some varieties, if left unpruned, will reach 9 or 10 feet tall in warm areas.

Polyantha   The late nineteenth century saw the introduction of the polyantha, a cross between the Asian *R. multiflora* and hybrid teas. These low-growing plants (most grow to 2 feet, although some can reach 5 feet) are ideal for mass plantings and low hedges. *Polyantha* is derived from the Greek word for "many-flowered," and these roses live up to their name, producing a great quantity of small flowers in clusters from late spring through the fall. Polyanthas are much hardier than hybrid teas, and their finely textured, narrow leaves also show the parentage of *R. multiflora*. The flowers are single, semidouble, or double, sometimes scented, in white, red, yellow, orange, and pastel shades of pink. The popularity of polyanthas was eclipsed by their more spectacular progeny, the floribunda roses. Today polyanthas are rarely grown.

Hybrid tea 'Duet' was grafted onto a sturdy trunk to form an elegant tree rose.

plant bests both the parents, however: It may grow to 6 feet or even taller in warm climates, making a grand background border. The blooms are usually double, borne either singly or in small clusters, without a striking fragrance, in solid colors of red, white, pink, orange, and yellow, as well as blends and dramatic bicolors.

Tree Roses

Sometimes called standard roses, tree roses are not a separate class of roses, but they are considered a distinct garden form. Almost any hybrid tea, floribunda, grandiflora, or miniature rose can be grown as a tree rose. Commercial growers graft the selected cultivar onto a tall, sturdy trunk of established rootstock to create this elegant form. The flower and foliage characteristics of a tree rose are those of the grafted cultivar.

Standards lend themselves to a variety of landscape uses, particularly in a formal or a traditional garden design. They usually need careful pruning (see page 58) to keep them symmetrical, round, and full. They also need protection against frost (see pages 53 and 54), except in mild-winter climates.

Miniature Roses

Thanks to miniature roses, anyone can find room for roses indoors or out. Miniature roses, or minis, as they are popularly called, usually grow 6 to 18 inches tall, although many of the newer varieties are considerably taller. The blooms of these delightful small plants are proportionately small: The perfect rose flower forms are retained in blooms ranging from a tiny ½ inch to 1½ inches wide.

Our knowledge about the antecedents of miniature roses is vague, but these roses probably derive from a Chinese native, *R. chinensis minima*, which was introduced in the West in the early 1900s. Miniature roses achieved a certain popularity at that time, when they were known as fairy flowers, but they disappeared from the market. Interest was rekindled in the 1920s, when tiny roses were discovered growing in a window box in a Swiss village. These were propagated and hybridized, and today there are hundreds of different varieties of miniature roses in bush form, as climbers, as standards, and with flowers in most colors and forms, even moss roses.

Floribunda   These roses combine the best qualities of their parents. They inherit flower form, medium-sized flowers, and foliage from the hybrid teas. From the polyanthas come increased hardiness, a low-growing habit (2 to 5 feet tall), and continuous bloom from late spring through fall. Clusters of flowers are borne on medium-length stems. Often fragrant, floribundas are available in a wide range of flower colors.

Grandiflora   Introduced in 1954, this group of roses is the result of crosses between hybrid teas and floribundas that again exploited the best qualities of both parents. The flower form and long stems are carried from the hybrid teas, and the increased hardiness and abundance of continuously blooming flowers are legacies of the floribunda. The flower size is midway between that of the two parents. The

Their compact size makes minis particularly suitable for edgings and for containers that can be easily moved. They are quite frost hardy; in severe climates they can be moved to shelter or covered. Minis can also be grown indoors (see page 63).

Climbing Roses

Climbing roses have been used for centuries to cover walls, trellises, pergolas, and walkways. They bring the beauty and fragrance of the rose to eye and nose level, flooding the senses. Climbing roses are divided into two groups: large-flowered climbers, which have rigid, thick canes; and ramblers, which have thinner, flexible canes.

Large-flowered climbers These plants do not strictly climb, since they have no tendrils or other means to secure themselves. Most of them are simply tall plants that need to be loosely secured to some support. Some climbers have canes that are rigid and strong enough to support themselves to heights of 10 feet, but they are traditionally tied to a pillar or a post so that they will not snap off in high winds. These are known as pillar roses.

Large-flowered climbers produce 10- to 15-foot canes, which carry the flowers in clusters. The blossoms can be 2 to 6 inches across, in a wide range of forms and colors. Most large-flowered climbers bloom twice, in the late spring or early summer and again in the fall. They are relatively hardy and somewhat resistant to disease.

Large-flowered climbers take about two growing seasons before they bloom. They should not be pruned during these first two years. (See pages 57 and 58 for instructions on pruning climbing roses.)

Climbing roses can be grown upward on pillars and arbors or horizontally along fences. Large-flowered climber 'Don Juan' produces a bounty of heavily scented, scarlet flowers throughout the growing season.

There are climbing versions of hybrid teas and their descendants and of polyanthas and miniatures. These are sports; the flowers and foliage resemble the original, but they are often less hardy and bear fewer blooms.

There is also a modern group of climbers and semiclimbers that are actually classified as shrubs. This is the kordesii class, developed by the German breeder Wilhelm Kordes in the 1950s. The plants grow to 6 to 12 feet, are very hardy, and produce flowers in clusters throughout the summer and fall. 'Dortmund', which has 2½- to 3½-inch single red flowers with white centers, is a popular cultivar in this group.

Ramblers These roses have very long (10- to 20-foot) slender canes that bear thick clusters of small flowers less than 2 inches across. As long as a rambler has something to lean on, it grows with abandon. Ramblers bloom only once, but the lack of repeat bloom is more than compensated for by the breathtaking profusion of blossoms in late spring or early summer. Ramblers are extremely hardy but tend to be susceptible to powdery mildew if there is inadequate air circulation around the foliage. Blossoms are semidouble or double, in red, pale pink, white, or yellow.

THE DEVELOPMENT OF NEW ROSES

The development of new and improved roses has been constant, for centuries. There is no reason to believe that this quest for new flower colors and forms, continuous blooms, increased hardiness, and disease resistance will abate. But it is difficult to predict what the favorite rose of the future will be. Yet-untried or even unthought-of crosses may produce hybrids of unexpectedly high quality or beautiful form. Fashion, a notoriously fickle arbitrator, also plays a large role in the development of roses.

It is likely, however, that radically new roses will be the offspring of crosses made with species roses that have not yet been the subject of experimentation. These crosses will produce new foliage forms, flower forms, colors, cultural requirements, and degrees of disease resistance. Many rosarians and breeders believe that such crosses are necessary if the rose is to keep its crown as "queen of the flowers." The extensive inbreeding of the hybrid teas and their descendants has now reached the point where

increasing numbers of roses, instead of fewer, are delicate and susceptible to disease. The rose of the future is perhaps being developed by dedicated breeders like the Kordes family in Germany and Sam McGredy in New Zealand, who have done extensive work with crosses of the Scotch rose (*R. spinosissima*).

Some hybridizers strive for a particular goal, releasing several new cultivars with similar characteristics. One such group is composed of the David Austin roses, named for its British originator. Austin's roses resemble old garden roses, but they are everblooming. They are hardy and very floriferous, with the appearance and fragrance of old garden roses. Some varieties are 'Otello', 'Wife of Bath', 'The Reeve', 'Fair Bianca', and 'The Squire'.

Another such group has been developed by the House of Meilland, the famous French breeders who developed 'Peace' and many other hybrid teas, grandifloras, and floribundas. The Meideland roses are designed to be the perfect landscape roses—easy to grow, needing little attention or pruning, and disease resistant. They can be sheared as hedges, and they are even resistant to highway salts when planted in median strips. They bloom heavily in massive clusters. 'Bonica', the 1987 All-America Rose Selections (AARS) winner, is the best known of this group. Other cultivars are 'Sevillana', 'White Meideland', 'Scarlet Meideland', and 'Pink Meideland'.

Up until the mid-nineteenth century, hybridizing was a rather haphazard process. For many years the mistaken belief persisted that a rose inherited its primary characteristics from the seed parent, and the pollen parent had little influence. It is now known that products of crosses take characteristics without favoritism from both the pollen parent and the seed parent. Which characteristics will be carried by the offspring and which will be rejected is the gamble in every cross. Complete and accurate records were seldom kept, and it is now close to impossible to determine the ancestry of most early hybrids.

Modern hybridizers keep careful records and take advantage of current botanical and genetic knowledge. Add to this a dose of imagination, persistence, and a large measure of good luck, and you have a rose breeder's qualifications. Most of the roses available now have been produced by about fifty professional

A climbing polyantha trained over the entry gate welcomes visitors to the garden.

Top left: Each yellow tag in this hybridizing greenhouse represents a cross.
Top center: The results of the work.
Top right: The miniatures are planted in the ground, and their progress is monitored.
Bottom: The result of breeding: new miniatures for fanciers.

hybridizers in about a dozen countries. In the course of developing new cultivars, each of these hybridizers cross-pollinates literally thousands of roses a year, collecting tens of thousands of seeds. The number of possible new genetic combinations is immense; however, the odds are about 10,000 to 1 against any specific cross-fertilization producing an outstanding new rose.

The development of new roses is not left entirely in the hands of the professionals. Those fifty or so professional breeders are joined by numerous amateurs, some of whom beat the odds and produce an award-winning and commercially successful rose. If you'd like to try hybridizing, the step-by-step instructions on pages 59 to 61 will help you get started.

Testing

A rose hybridizer must be patient. From the time a promising rose is developed, 10 years or more may pass before the rose is introduced to the public. A rose company may evaluate seedlings from as many as 600 different new roses each year. Ninety-five percent of them originate within the company or come from professional hybridizers. From this initial cull, 25 to 30 will be deemed worthy of further observation. Of these, a dozen or so are kept for more trials, which may last as long as five years. After this, only four or five will be chosen for public introduction.

Since introducing roses to the public represents a considerable investment in growing space, time, labor, and promotion, the commercial rose nurseries must select those that will do well in all the varied and sometimes extreme climates across North America. To this end, they field-test the roses in test gardens throughout the United States.

During these years of testing, the flowers are rated on such factors as petal count, form, resistance to rain, color, repeat bloom, and fragrance. Disease resistance, hardiness, foliage, and growth habit are also judged. A rose that does well in most categories will be marketed.

Patents

Until the passage of the Townsend-Purnell Plant Patent Act in 1930, a hybridizer could invest in the development of a new rose and then reap few rewards. As soon as a plant was released, it could be propagated by anyone.

The Plant Patent Act protects newly developed plants in the same way that industrial inventions are protected. The patent owner is given proprietary rights to the plant for 17 years. During that time the owner is entitled to a royalty for every offspring of the plant. Thus, the rose hybridizer can recoup development costs and perhaps even make a little profit. Commercial rose nurseries often purchase licenses from the hybridizers to propagate and sell particular cultivars.

The law requires that all patented roses be identified by a patent number engraved on a tag attached to the plant. Do not buy roses sold as patented unless they carry this identification tag. It is your guarantee that the plant will perform as the cultivar advertised.

Cultivar Names

Before a rose is ready for its public debut, it needs a name. The hybridizer or distributing nursery chooses the name and, in the United States, registers it with the American Rose Society, designated by the International Horticultural Congress as the International Registration Authority for Roses (IRAR). Names too similar to existing botanical or cultivar names are rejected. A name can be reused after 30 years if there is proof that the original rose is extinct, is not of historical importance, and is not a parent of an existing cultivar.

ROSE SOCIETIES

Many gardeners who are captivated by roses and develop a special interest in them want to share their triumphs and problems with fellow rosarians. They also want to know of new cultivars and new pest-control techniques and products, and to keep up-to-date on which roses in the marketplace are garnering the top awards. Rose societies offer these benefits and more to the interested gardener.

The American Rose Society

This society boasts more than 30,000 members, mostly amateurs, making it the largest special plant society in the United States. There are more than 380 local chapters and affiliated rose societies throughout the United States. At its headquarters in Shreveport, Louisiana, the society has established The American Rose Center, a 118-acre park planted extensively with roses. Members receive the monthly *American Rose* magazine and the *American Rose Annual,* a book that contains scientific information on roses and rose growing and articles of general interest to rose lovers.

For more information, contact the American Rose Society, Box 30,000, Shreveport, LA 71130 (318-938-5402).

The Heritage Roses Group

Formed in 1975, the Heritage Roses Group is a fellowship for those who grow and enjoy old roses. Members receive *The Rose Letter* quarterly, which contains articles of interest on old roses, sources of plants, and cultural tips. A membership list is available for a small fee so that you may contact other group members in your area.

Annual dues are $5 for members in the United States and $6 for those in Canada or Mexico. For membership, write to Miriam Wilkins, 925 Galvin Street, El Cerrito, CA 94530.

An All-America Rose Selection in 1967, hybrid tea 'Bewitched' is still widely grown for its exquisite pink blooms and spicy fragrance.

Roses in the Landscape

Roses can perform almost any landscaping job in the garden. Here's how to choose healthy, vigorous plants of the right type and variety to assure years of pleasure.

Roses are among the most versatile plants available to gardeners. Don't shortchange them by thinking of them simply as bloom-producing machines; they can be an effective and integral part of a successful landscape design. Because of the wide variety in their growth habits and sizes, roses can meet almost any landscaping challenge. And, unlike some other perennials, roses bloom the first year they're planted, so you won't have to wait long before enjoying their colorful displays.

Use low-growing floribundas or miniatures to edge a walkway, or create a mass of summer color by filling a bed with hybrid teas. Many types of roses make excellent foundation plantings; you can match or contrast them with the color of your house. Climbers trained on a trellis provide privacy; grown against the house, they can cover an awkward architectural feature or frame a window or door. Shrub and species roses, as well as the stately grandifloras, make excellent background plantings or tall hedges. Roses demand good drainage, so they are especially suitable for terraced hillsides. The smaller roses adapt well to container gardening, which means you can move them around to create striking effects. Miniatures grown inside will provide flowers all year around.

It's unfortunate that roses aren't used more predominantly in landscaping; no other plant produces so many flowers so reliably over so long a period of time or has such an astounding variety of growth habits and flower forms.

Different types of roses can perform many landscape functions. In this rose garden, roses grow up an arbor that greets visitors, show off as specimen plants inside, and screen the shed.

'Paul's Scarlet Climber' creates a dramatic focal point for this house.

effect. It may be more convenient to have all the roses in one area when you are pruning, watering, and fertilizing them. But as long as the site is right (a topic to be discussed in a moment), there's no reason not to enjoy roses in all parts of the garden, as a focal point or as part of a colorful tapestry with other plants.

Miniatures are particularly versatile; they will fit in well with all parts of the garden and provide gorgeous spots of color. Use them as an edging around flower beds or the vegetable garden, or mix them with low-growing annuals, such as alyssum, calendula, and viola, or with small rock-garden plants.

Roses can be an integral part of a formal or an informal garden design. A formal design is characterized by symmetry and straight or regularly curving lines. Elegant tree roses are an excellent choice for a formal garden: A row of them can seem like a colorful guard of honor at attention. An informal garden is more natural and asymmetrical. Graceful, arching shrub roses and climbers cascading over a wall or arbor are at home in an informal landscape.

There is a type of garden planned for efficiency, without regard to design considerations. This is the cutting garden, usually located in an out-of-the-way part of the yard, where flowers are raised for shows or indoor arrangements. Roses in a cutting garden can be given optimum spacing and arranged so that they can be cared for conveniently.

One of the key words in landscaping is *restraint.* A specimen plant is one that is particularly lovely or spectacular and is allowed to stand alone or to dominate part of a landscape. A single strategically placed rosebush can be a bold accent that serves as a focal point. When a rose stands alone or is positioned to stand out among other plants, it should be special, with exceptional blooms, fragrance, or foliage.

Planting Sites

There are four considerations to keep in mind when you are choosing a spot in the garden to plant a rose: exposure to sun and to wind, type of soil, and neighboring plants.

Sun Roses should receive at least six hours of full sun a day. In areas with intense summer heat, they will appreciate some shade in the afternoon when the sun is hottest. A rose

DESIGNING YOUR GARDEN

Many gardeners elect to keep all their rose plants in one part of the garden. The tradition of a separate rose garden stems from the nineteenth-century practice of devoting an extensive section to roses, another section to herbs, a third to water plants, and so forth. A mass of roses can produce a stunning and harmonious

will grow in shade, but it will be spindly and unattractive, and it will produce fewer blossoms. The plant's susceptibility to rust and powdery mildew also increases in shade.

Wind   Don't plant roses in exposed locations where they will be subjected to prevailing strong winds. Wind damages blossoms and causes rapid evaporation of moisture from the foliage, making it necessary to water the plants more often. Consider planting trees or shrubs to shield your roses if you have a windy site.

Soil   Roses do best in slightly acid soil, but generally they will grow reasonably well in all but the most extreme soil types. The soil must be well drained and at the same time retain moisture for use by the roots. If you don't have well-drained soil in your garden, either bring in new soil and create a raised bed or amend the soil to create better drainage (see pages 37 and 38).

A hillside provides good drainage and helps to show off the roses, too. Make terraces, with a path on each terrace for tending and admiring the roses.

Competition   Roses should not be planted too close to large trees or shrubs whose roots will compete with them for water and nutrients. If you need to, bury header boards 2 to 3 feet below the surface to keep the tree or shrub roots from encroaching on the roses. Some of the larger shrub roses do not need this protection, because they develop extensive root systems.

No English cottage garden is complete without roses. Wonderfully fragrant old-garden roses are particularly suited to this style of landscaping.

Top: Climber 'Golden Showers' brightens a rustic post fence. Right: An All-America Rose Selection in 1984, floribunda 'Intrigue' is valued for its unusual deep plum blossoms and old-fashioned fragrance.

Layout

After identifying the appropriate places for planting roses in the garden, start thinking about the type, size, and number of rose plants you can accommodate. If you want to plant one or two roses among other plants, consider the eventual size of the rose and the mature size of the neighboring plants (if they are not fully grown). Allow enough space so that the rose plant will receive plenty of sun and sufficient air circulation around it even when it's fully grown. Remember that some of the old roses and shrub roses are very vigorous.

If you're thinking about more than one or two roses, whether in a separate section of the garden or in just a single bed, it's helpful to sketch to scale a plan of the planting area. Then you won't need to continually prune the roses to keep them far enough apart or to move the overcrowded plants later on.

Size The chart on this page shows the approximate heights the different classes of roses reach when mature. These are not iron-clad limits by any means: How tall roses grow depends on the climate and how heavily the plants are pruned. Within the same class there are also variations in growth. Hybrid teas, for example, include low-, moderate-, and tall-growing cultivars.

Don't plant tall-growing cultivars in front of lower-growing ones. If you do, you won't be able to enjoy the ones hidden in the back. That may seem like an obvious admonition, but it's an easy mistake to make in the excitement of planning and planting.

As a rule of thumb, figure the spread of a rosebush to be about two thirds its height. As mentioned earlier, good air circulation around a plant lessens the likelihood of disease. Remember to allow plenty of room between two different cultivars; they can look unkempt when entangled with each other. If you are planting more than one row of roses, stagger the plants in neighboring rows. This improves air circulation and provides a less rigid appearance.

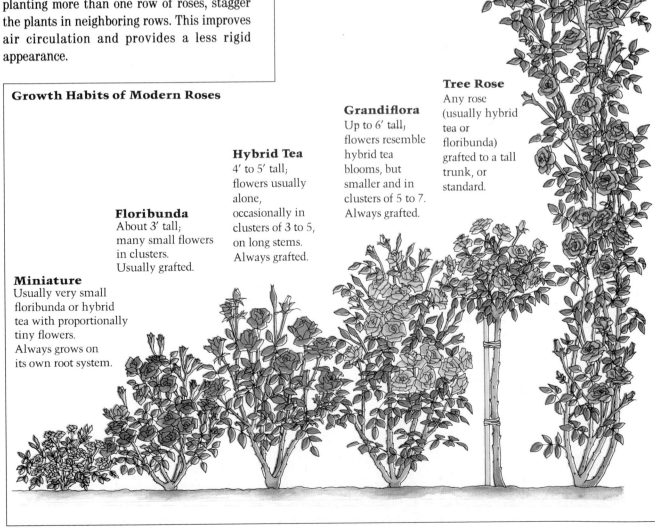

Growth Habits of Modern Roses

Climber
6′ to 20′ tall; usually grown on a fence, trellis, or post. Some are grafted.

Tree Rose
Any rose (usually hybrid tea or floribunda) grafted to a tall trunk, or standard.

Grandiflora
Up to 6′ tall; flowers resemble hybrid tea blooms, but smaller and in clusters of 5 to 7. Always grafted.

Hybrid Tea
4′ to 5′ tall; flowers usually alone, occasionally in clusters of 3 to 5, on long stems. Always grafted.

Floribunda
About 3′ tall; many small flowers in clusters. Usually grafted.

Miniature
Usually very small floribunda or hybrid tea with proportionally tiny flowers. Always grows on its own root system.

Modern shrub rose
'Nevada' makes an
appealing screen or
background planting.

If you won't be able to tend the roses from a path, leave a little extra room between the plants so that you can move among them without being continually grabbed by thorns. Stay well clear of the base of the plants in order not to compact the soil and inhibit water drainage. Plant the rosebushes at least 2 feet back from walkways so thorny branches won't snag passersby.

Color Many gardeners believe that all roses blend together, but others prefer a careful plan that avoids clashing colors and creates a harmonious effect. Roses provide a long seasonal parade of color, so plan a look you'll enjoy. Your preferences and imagination are the only limits here.

You may choose a monochromatic scheme, planting roses of a single color or several shades of one color. If you locate the roses near the house, choose a hue that blends well with the materials or color of your house.

Some gardeners prefer carefully planned arrangements of two or three colors. Try yellows and oranges together, or pinks and reds. You can also design with two contrasting colors, such as lavender and orange, or yellow and violet.

Mixed colors lose their effectiveness in small areas, so it's usually best to plant at least several bushes of the same color. In a large space you can use bold splashes of color in every hue, but plant at least two roses of the same color together so there will be small blocks of different colors rather than little spots. In this manner, you can create a riot of color, which can be tempered with a white rose.

Most blooms are best highlighted against a background of dark greenery or a fence or wall painted a dark color. However, plants with deep pink blossoms need a light backdrop to display their rich colors to the best advantage. Colors can also be used to make a garden seem smaller or larger than it really is. Bright, warm colors like scarlet, orange, and yellow planted at the rear of a garden will make the space appear smaller; cool colors like maroon, violet, and lavender will make it seem longer or deeper.

For help in planning a successful layout, refer to the lists of cultivars arranged by color starting on page 102.

Left: With its long-lasting clusters of pure white flowers, floribunda 'Iceberg' makes an excellent hedge or border. Bottom: Two floribundas, 'Deep Purple' and 'Sunsprite', create a handsome bicolored border. Both are delightfully scented, especially 'Sunsprite', a recipient of the James Alexander Gamble Rose Fragrance Medal.

Roses in Containers

Planting in containers allows the gardener even more flexibility for integrating roses into the landscape. Container-grown roses can be placed almost anywhere and, of course, are easily repositioned if desired.

For a special party, frame your entryway with roses in pots. Enjoy spots of color and fragrance with roses on the patio or deck. Create colorful window-box displays with individually potted miniature roses. Bring color to eye level with hanging baskets of roses.

Containers are also a boon to gardeners who live in apartments or townhouses and don't have ground to work in. Don't forget that miniatures can be grown indoors in a bright, sunny window or under artificial lights.

Small hybrid teas, standards, floribundas, polyanthas, and miniatures are the best roses for small containers. Floribundas and polyanthas produce blooms in clusters, giving the effect of large sweeps of color. Large hybrid teas, grandifloras, and most old roses are better in large containers (5 gallons and up).

In cold-winter areas, gardeners can transport large pots and planters on a dolly or a small platform with casters to a sheltered and heated location for protection. Gardeners in warmer climates may want to move their containers to an inconspicuous part of the garden when the roses are dormant.

CHOOSING A ROSE

After deciding on location, plant size, and color scheme, it's time to select varieties. There is an astounding array of plants available in almost every conceivable combination of characteristics. Nearly two hundred and fifty different roses are listed on pages 72 to 101. Don't be overwhelmed by the large number; once you've decided on the characteristics you want in a rose, the list becomes more manageable.

Characteristics to Consider

When you are making your choice, there are a number of questions to ask yourself: How much time will I have to care for the plants? How much winter protection will they need in my climate? Is fragrance an important criterion? Do I want color in the garden or flowers to cut for indoor arrangements? Will different shades of color go together as well as I think?

Maintenance   All roses need some care, but certain ones need substantially less than others. On page 107 is a list of roses that can thrive with a minimum of care. If you wish to explore beyond this listing, pick varieties that are particularly disease resistant. That way you won't have to worry about being eternally vigilant about the control and prevention of disease. To reduce maintenance, be sure to give the plants described as vigorous ample room to grow; otherwise you'll always need to have your pruning clippers at the ready.

Disease resistance   The particular resistance—or susceptibility—of a plant to some or all diseases is noted in the Encyclopedia of Roses beginning on page 71. Resistant roses may be attacked, but it's unlikely they will develop the disease. Plants that are described as being susceptible, or that have no notation about resistance, will not necessarily succumb to disease, although you probably should take precautions (see page 48).

Certain diseases are often concentrated in certain areas. Talk to friends and neighbors who grow roses about their experiences to determine whether a particular disease is troublesome in your area. Or seek the counsel of your local rose society members. On page 107 is a list of roses that are especially resistant to disease.

Climate   Find out what the usual coldest winter temperatures are in your area. In severe winter climates you will need to provide some protection for roses (see pages 52 to 54), but even if you plan to protect them, don't choose plants described as very tender—that is, unable to withstand freezing temperatures. Some roses perform well where summers are hot and dry, others where summers are hot and humid, or cool. If a rose has special climate requirements, they are noted in the Encyclopedia of Roses beginning on page 71. Also refer to the list of hardiest roses (those able to survive very cold weather) on page 107.

Fragrance   Most people who pause to admire a rose will first lean over and take a sniff. If the rose is fragrant, the enjoyment seems to be complete. If fragrance is a large part of your pleasure in roses, there are many roses you can choose from. 'Chrysler Imperial'

Miniature 'Cupcake' adds subtle beauty to a deck or patio.

Public gardens provide a wealth of ideas for home landscaping.

and 'Fragrant Cloud', two very popular hybrid teas, are exceptionally fragrant; among the old roses, many of the damasks are noted for their fragrance. A selection of fragrant roses is given on page 106.

Cut flowers You'll probably want to cut some of your flowers and bring them inside to enjoy. (See pages 66 and 67 for procedures to assure their longevity.) All roses can be picked for indoor arrangements, but hybrid teas and grandifloras are favored for formal arrangements because of their long, straight stems. A list of varieties that produce long-lasting blossoms for indoor arrangements is given on pages 106 and 107.

Colors Remember that within any one color classification, such as red or gold, there is a wide range of intensity and quality of color. When juxtaposing or blending different colors, make sure that the shades you choose will give the effect you desire.

Public Rose Gardens
You can learn a great deal from visits to public rose gardens. There you can pick up landscaping

ideas, see new introductions and roses that are being field-tested, appreciate unusual or hard-to-find varieties, and study old-fashioned cultivars. Keep in mind that the roses in a particular garden are responding to the climate and other growing conditions of that site. They may not do as well in your garden if conditions are less favorable.

Look for roses you like. Observe their growth to see whether they will fit your landscaping needs. Let specimen blooms guide you in selecting color, fragrance, and size. Jot down the names so that later you can order or find the species or cultivar that is exactly what you want. A resident horticulturist is usually happy to answer questions.

Many commercial rose growers and retailers have display gardens that are open to the public. In addition to visiting local gardens, consult the listing of rose sources on page 108. It's always best to call ahead first.

Rose Shows
Local chapters of the American Rose Society (ARS) hold frequent local and regional shows in which members compete for awards. You won't be able to inspect the plants, but you will be able to observe and smell many near-perfect flowers. You will also have a chance to get information and opinions from experienced rose gardeners. Write to the national society office (see page 21) for information on your local chapter.

Awards and Ratings
Some other guides for selecting varieties are the ratings and awards given to roses. Award-winning and top-rated roses are sure to be exceptional in a number of performance categories.

All-America Rose Selections After the passage of the Plant Patent Act in 1930, large numbers of roses, some of very poor quality, were patented and sold to the public. To supply the rose-buying public with objective data on the best new introductions, the major rose growers in 1938 formed a nonprofit group, All-America Rose Selections (AARS), to recognize outstanding new introductions.

Each new introduction is subjected to rigorous, standardized observation over a two-year period in 23 test gardens in the varied climates of the United States. Judges rate each rose under submission according to 14 different categories: novelty, bud form, flower form, color on opening, color at end of bloom, substance (texture of the petals), fragrance, flower stem or cluster formation, growth habit, vigor, foliage, disease resistance, flowering effect, and overall value. The roses with the highest rating are then declared the winners. Many of the AARS winners for the last 15 years, plus some older favorites, are included in the Encyclopedia of Roses starting on page 71.

The AARS also distributes to affiliated public rose gardens new introductions the year before they are listed in catalogs, which allows you to inspect new roses in bloom the year that they are introduced.

American Rose Society ratings Every three years the ARS surveys its membership in all parts of the United States for their ratings on the roses they've grown. Varieties and cultivars are rated on a scale of 1 to 10, and the results are published annually in the *Handbook for Selecting Roses* (see page 21 for information on obtaining a copy). The ARS breaks down the ratings qualitatively in the following ranges:

10.0	Perfect (not yet achieved)
9.0–9.9	Outstanding
8.0–8.9	Excellent
7.0–7.9	Good
6.0–6.9	Fair
5.9 and lower	Of questionable value

Keep in mind that a low rating does not necessarily mean that the rose is a dud. It may still have many fine attributes that make it worth growing, such as fragrance or hardiness, although other characteristics are less than perfect. Scores may also be low because the rose doesn't do as well in some geographical areas as it does in others. A low-rated rose may do extremely well in your region but fail in others. Ratings are provided for the roses listed in the Encyclopedia of Roses beginning on page 71.

Other awards The Gold Medal Certificate was established by the ARS in 1948 to recognize those roses that have shown the best performance over a period of five years. To date,

only 13 have been chosen: from the hybrid teas, 'Chrysler Imperial', 'Peace', and 'Tropicana'; from the grandifloras, 'Carrousel', 'Montezuma', and 'Queen Elizabeth'; from the floribundas, 'Fashion', 'Frensham', 'Spartan', and 'Vogue'; and representing the large-flowered climbers, shrubs, and miniatures, 'City of York', 'Golden Wings', and 'Toy Clown', respectively. Not all of these are included in the Encyclopedia of Roses; although they were outstanding when first introduced, some have been eclipsed by other, superior varieties.

In 1961 Dr. James Alexander Gamble established a fund with the ARS to encourage the development of fragrant roses. The James Alexander Gamble Rose Fragrance Medal is awarded to roses with a nationwide rating of 8.0 or better that are "strongly and delightfully fragrant." Thus far, fewer than a dozen roses have been judged worthy of this prize. Winners of the award are indicated in the list of fragrant roses on page 106.

The ARS sponsors an Award of Excellence for miniature roses. This was established in the mid-1970s in recognition of the increasing popularity of miniatures. The listing of minis on pages 98 to 101 includes many winners.

Every All-America Rose Selection— including 'Tournament of Roses', a grandiflora selected in 1988—undergoes extensive testing.

Planting and Caring for Roses

If you follow the simple techniques of planting and regular care outlined here, your efforts will be amply rewarded by productive, healthy plants.

This chapter is a summary of techniques for caring for roses. It is not gospel. If you bring 10 rosarians together, it's more than likely that you will get 10 different answers to a question on a particular cultural practice. All the answers will be valid for each gardener and his or her garden. You will find the methods that work best for you and your garden through experience—including, probably, a few failures.

Roses can survive neglect and even abuse, but the results will not be pleasing: a few small blossoms supported by ratty, tangled foliage. A rosebush with a full quota of clean, healthy leaves and a constant supply of moisture and nutrients will produce more than twice as many blooms as one scantily fed and only partially protected from pests, diseases, and the elements.

Climbing roses trained on a post-and-chain fence create an unusual and spectacular effect.

Check the roots and canes before buying bare-root roses.

CHOOSING HEALTHY PLANTS

To get off to a good start with rose plants, it pays to spend time and effort—and sometimes a little more money—to choose healthy, vigorous plants that will perform to their full potential.

Rose plants are available either bare-root or growing in containers. Either type of plant, if carefully chosen, will produce good roses over a long lifetime. The best bet is to purchase plants from reputable mail-order suppliers or local nurseries. You'll be buying from people who sell roses year after year and stand behind the quality of their plants. Be cautious of bargains, especially those offered by retail stores in which nursery plants are a sideline. The plants have probably had less-than-perfect care, and they may be permanently damaged. You will be making a considerable investment of time and energy in each rose plant, so it's advisable to spend a little extra money for quality.

Buying Container-Grown Plants

Container-grown plants have a couple of advantages over bare-root plants: They are growing and sometimes blooming, so you can see what the roses look like and whether they are fragrant. Container roses are also somewhat easier to plant. However, they are generally more expensive than bare-root plants, and fewer varieties are available.

When buying a container-grown plant, examine the foliage and canes carefully. The plant should look healthy and vigorous. There should be no dieback or twiggy growth, evidence that it has been growing in the container for over a year.

Container-grown roses are often available throughout the year in nurseries, but it's best not to buy them after midsummer, when it is more difficult to establish plants in the garden and when the plants may have become pot-bound. Steer clear of roses planted in small (less than 5-gallon) pots, as the roots may have been severely pruned to fit the small container.

Miniature roses are almost always sold in containers. They can be safely bought throughout the year, since they are often grown in greenhouses and started at different times of the year. Select plants with healthy green foliage that is not tangled.

Buying Bare-Root Plants

Bare-root roses are shipped and sold while the plants are dormant and need only to be kept cool and moist. All mail-order suppliers ship bare-root plants; they will deliver them at the best planting time for your area or whenever you specify.

Bare-root rose plants are graded as 1, 1½, or 2, based on the size and number of canes. If you're willing to pay for the best possible blooms, buy number 1 grade plants with three or four heavy canes at least ⅜ inch in diameter and 18 inches long on hybrid teas and grandifloras or 15 inches long on floribundas. To meet the number 1 grade, these roses must have at least two canes of the specified length, and branching must begin no more than 3 inches above the bud union. Number 1 polyanthas must have at least four canes 12 inches or longer. Climbers must have at least three canes 24 inches or longer to qualify for the top grade.

Nurseries usually keep bare-root plants in boxes of moist sawdust, so you can inspect the roots as well as the canes. The root system should be sturdy and fibrous, with several firm, well-branched roots. Make sure that the canes are not dry and shriveled; they should be firm, plump, and green. The plant should be well shaped, with no symptoms of disease such as deformed growth, abnormal swellings, or discolorations on the canes or roots.

Rose growers often wrap the canes in plastic so that they retain their moisture. However, the plastic acts as a greenhouse, encouraging the plants to start growing. As soon as you get the rose plants home, remove the plastic from around the canes and store the plants as described below. If the canes do start to sprout before they're planted, pinch back the shoots to ¼ inch to prevent the moisture from evaporating.

Storing bare-root plants   Bare-root plants should be kept cool and moist until they are planted. They must be kept moist or they will die; if they aren't kept cool, they will begin to grow and there will be a greater risk of injuring the foliage and roots when they are planted.

If the ground is not frozen and it can be worked, heel bare-root plants into a trench.

Dig a trench in a shady spot with one sloping side, and lay the plant on the sloping side with the roots at the bottom of the trench. Cover both the roots and the canes with soil and water it thoroughly.

Alternatively, you can store your plants with the roots packed in a moisture-retaining material such as sawdust, peat moss, or perlite. Keep them in a cool, but not freezing, place, and make sure the material remains damp; if it dries out, soak it in water and then squeeze out the excess moisture. Wet newspapers or burlap laid over the canes will further reduce evaporation from the plants.

PREPARING THE SITE

Roses perform best when they receive full sunshine all day, or at least six hours of direct sunlight daily, from spring through fall. Morning sun is essential; partial afternoon shade is acceptable.

There should be air movement through the foliage to keep it dry and to discourage disease. Plant roses away from large trees or shrubs that might compete for nutrients, moisture, and sunlight.

Improving Drainage

Roses need good drainage. If your site doesn't drain well, you can modify it in several ways.

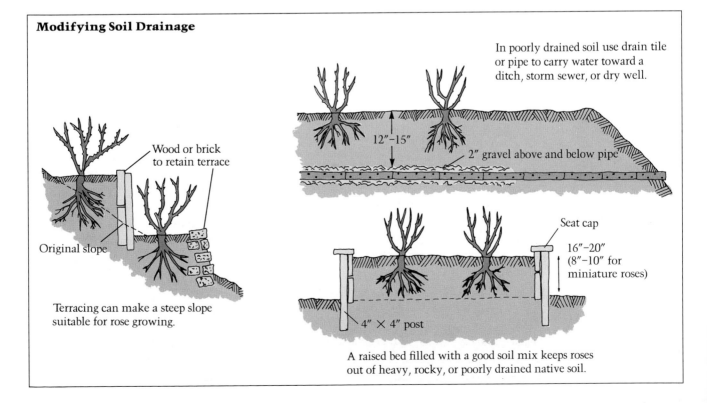

Modifying Soil Drainage

Wood or brick to retain terrace

Original slope

Terracing can make a steep slope suitable for rose growing.

In poorly drained soil use drain tile or pipe to carry water toward a ditch, storm sewer, or dry well.

12″–15″

2″ gravel above and below pipe

Seat cap

16″–20″
(8″–10″ for miniature roses)

4″ × 4″ post

A raised bed filled with a good soil mix keeps roses out of heavy, rocky, or poorly drained native soil.

Drain tile or pipe If you are preparing a large rose bed, you can dig a trench and bury drain tile or pipe in coarse gravel 12 to 15 inches beneath the planting site. Cover the drain openings with asphalt roofing paper or a filter fabric to prevent soil from washing in and clogging the holes. Slightly slant the pipe toward a ditch, a storm sewer, or a dry well.

Raised beds An easier solution is to build a raised bed. In very moist areas, build a bed at least 16 to 20 inches high. Beds for miniature roses can be half as high. The sides can be redwood or masonry framing, old railway ties, or even stone or brick. Fill the bed with a soil mix made according to the directions below. In addition to providing excellent drainage, raised beds are a convenient height for gardening chores.

In severe-winter climates, be sure to plant the roses at least 12 inches from the side of a raised bed; the soil will act as insulation for the roots.

Terraces Slopes usually have excellent drainage, but soil erosion may be a problem. Terracing, which creates level surfaces on a hillside, helps prevent erosion. It also turns an unusable steep slope into one suitable for rose growing. The terraces allow water to soak into the root zone of plants instead of washing down the hill. You can use wood, stone, or brick to retain a terrace.

Amending the Soil

Although roses do well in a wide range of soils, they prefer loamy soil with a high humus content to a depth of at least 2 feet. The following mix is an ideal growing medium for raised beds and terraces:

> 5 parts (by volume) loamy soil
> 4 parts organic matter, such as compost or leaf mold, dehydrated cow manure, peat moss, or shredded bark
> 1 part builder's sand

Add 3 to 4 pounds of superphosphate per 100 square feet for stronger root development.

If you're planting bushes individually and the soil is good, dig holes 16 to 20 inches wide and 14 to 18 inches deep. Work organic matter and sand into the excavated soil, which will be used to backfill the holes. Use the same

principle for a large bed of roses. For best results, most experts advise preparing the soil three to six months before planting the roses.

If you have extremely poor soil, remove all existing soil in the planting bed to a depth of 16 to 20 inches, and replace it with a mixture of good loam, sand, and organic matter in the proportions given here.

Roses grow best in a slightly acid soil, with a pH of 6.0 to 6.5. If you suspect that your soil is alkaline, perform a soil test. If the soil is too alkaline, make it more acidic by working in agricultural sulfur. How much to add depends on the texture of the soil: To lower the pH of 100 square feet of soil by 1 point (from 7.5 to 6.5), apply 1 pound of sulfur to light, sandy loam, 1½ pounds to medium-weight loam, and 2 pounds to clay loam.

If your soil is very acidic (lower than pH 5.0), then liming to raise the pH is warranted. Regardless of the texture of the soil, add 5 to 8 pounds of ground limestone per 100 square feet to correct the problem.

If you are preparing a large planting bed and there have been problems with nematodes or soil-borne diseases in your area, it may be a good idea to fumigate the soil before you plant roses. Do not do this, however, unless a soil laboratory has diagnosed a problem that will be helped by fumigation. If so, a highly satisfactory fumigant is Vapam®, a liquid that works better under an airtight cover. Check with your local Cooperative Extension Agent about applying the fumigant.

PLANTING ROSES IN THE GARDEN

Roses bought in containers can be planted in the garden at any time of year when weather permits. It is best to plant in spring, or in fall in warm climates, so that the roots can establish themselves in your soil before they are stressed by heat. If you plant during hot weather, however, be sure to check vigilantly to make sure the rose has enough moisture for at least six weeks after planting. (For instructions on watering newly planted roses, see pages 45 and 46.)

Bare-root roses, on the other hand, are available only when the roses are dormant. Planting times vary according to the severity of the winter climate. If temperatures do not fall below 10° F in your area, you can plant

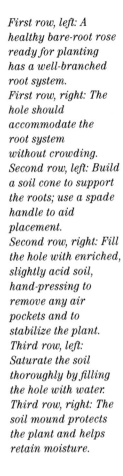

First row, left: A healthy bare-root rose ready for planting has a well-branched root system.
First row, right: The hole should accommodate the root system without crowding.
Second row, left: Build a soil cone to support the roots; use a spade handle to aid placement.
Second row, right: Fill the hole with enriched, slightly acid soil, hand-pressing to remove any air pockets and to stabilize the plant.
Third row, left: Saturate the soil thoroughly by filling the hole with water.
Third row, right: The soil mound protects the plant and helps retain moisture.

Fourth row, left: When the rose has produced 1 to 2 inches of new growth and frost danger has passed, begin to remove the soil from around the canes.
Fourth row, right: Wash away a bit of the mound at each watering.

Planting Bare-Root Roses

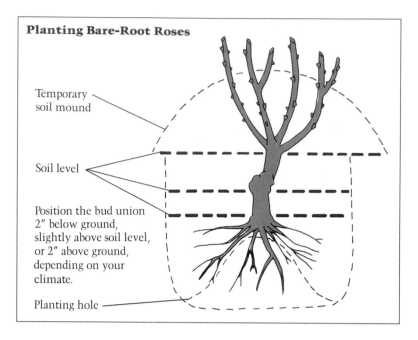

Temporary soil mound

Soil level

Position the bud union 2″ below ground, slightly above soil level, or 2″ above ground, depending on your climate.

Planting hole

whenever the dormant roses are available. If the minimum winter temperature is between 10° and -10° F, plant only in the early spring or late fall. If the coldest temperature in your region falls below -10° F, plant only in the early spring.

In cold-winter regions you can plant whenever the ground has thawed out enough to be worked easily. Generally, the best advice is to get a plant into the ground as early as possible to give the root system a head start before the foliage forms. But if you often get severe spring freezes, wait until the danger has passed. A newly planted young rose can be killed by a severe drop in temperature.

Don't plant bare-root roses on windy winter days when the temperature may drop below freezing. The combination of low temperatures and drying wind can be fatal to the tender new plants.

Planting Bare-Root Roses

Before planting, soak bare-root roses in water for a few hours (but no longer than 24 hours). Keep them in water until you are ready to plant. Trim any roots that have broken.

After preparing the hole as shown on the previous page, position the plant in the hole. The roots should not be twisted or curved. If one or two roots are too long for the hole, prune them back to 8 to 10 inches so that they will fit without being crowded.

Position the plant vertically by laying a spade handle or stake across the hole to align

the bud union—the knobby protuberance on the stem just below the canes, where the cultivar was grafted to the rootstock—with the level of the soil. The bud union is particularly sensitive to extreme cold, and its proper planting position is a point of disagreement among rosarians, even those within the same region. A rule of thumb is that it should be 2 inches below the soil in severe-winter areas (lows below -10° F), slightly above the soil in cold-winter areas (lows between 10° and -10° F), and 2 inches above the soil in mild-winter climates (lows above 10° F).

Build a cone of soil in the center of the hole to support the spread-out roots and to hold the plant at the right level. With the plant in position, fill the hole two thirds full with enriched soil, hand-pressing it to remove air pockets. Then fill the hole with water and let it soak in. Finish filling the hole with soil, firm it gently by hand, and settle it with a second soaking of water.

Mound the soil at least 8 inches high around the plant. You may need extra soil for this. Moisten again. This mound protects the plant from drying winds and warm sun and provides additional moisture a rose plant needs when it is developing.

Leave the mound intact until the new growth appearing at the tips of the canes is 1 or 2 inches long and all danger of frost has passed. Then gradually acclimate the plant by washing away a bit of the mound each day.

Bare-root tree roses should be securely staked after planting. Place the stake on the south side of the plant to partially shade the trunk, which is sensitive to hot sun.

Planting Container-Grown Roses

Dig a hole as deep as, and 5 to 6 inches wider than, the container in which the rose is growing. Remove the plant from the container. If it is a metal can, ask the nursery to slit the sides to make the plant easier to remove. If the bud union was incorrectly positioned when the rose was potted up, then reposition it in the hole. (See illustration above for correct placement.) Add soil around the rootball.

If the rose is not well rooted in the container, avoid disturbing the rootball. Cut out and remove the bottom of the container and carefully set the plant in the hole at the proper height. Cut the sides of the container and loosely fill the hole with soil. Remove the sides of the container and the container soil will remain intact around the roots. Water thoroughly to settle the soil, fill the hole with additional soil, and water again.

While the backfill soil is still wet and soupy, make final adjustments to the plant's position. If it is too deep, lift it, or tip it upright if it is leaning. Since the rose is already growing, there is no need to make a mound as in bare-root planting. Keep the plant well watered until it is established.

Transplanting Roses

Roses should be transplanted while they are dormant and the ground is workable. This will be late winter, early spring, or late fall, depending on your climate.

Prepare the new planting site as you would for planting a container-grown rose. Soak the soil around the plant overnight so you can move the plant with as much soil as possible to minimize root disturbance. Prune back large bushes by one half to make them easier to handle.

Move the rose to its new site and replant it immediately before the rootball dries out. Plant the rose as you would a container-grown rose. Position it in the new hole and firm the soil around the roots. Water the plant well and keep it adequately watered until the roots are established in the new site.

Planting Roses Grown in Containers

1. Dig a hole as deep as the container and 5" to 6" wider than it.

2. Remove plant from container and place it in the hole, making sure the bud union is at correct height for your climate.

3. Fill the hole loosely with soil, water thoroughly, refill the hole, and water again.

4. Keep plant well watered until it is established.

PLANTING ROSES IN CONTAINERS

Select a container that will give the root system ample room. Five-gallon nursery containers are the minimum size for most roses other than miniatures; most will grow much more lushly in larger containers. In a small pot a plant will become root-bound, which causes loss of leaves and poor flower production, and can even lead to death.

Wooden tubs and boxes are excellent for roses. Moisture can evaporate through the sides, and the soil stays cool. The common porous terra-cotta pots are simple, handsome, and readily available, but plants tend to dry out quicker in these than in glazed pottery. Plastic pots and metal containers, especially dark-colored ones, heat up in direct sun, causing the roots on the sunny side of the container to die.

Whatever your choice in containers, be sure to provide good drainage, or the roots of the plant may rot. It's advisable to have several holes in the bottom of the container. Cleats, casters, feet, wooden X's, or small pieces of brick positioned underneath the containers will keep the roots from standing in water and help prevent root rot.

Use a growing medium composed of 3 parts sandy loam and 1 part organic matter like peat moss or leaf mold. Most synthetic soil mixes available ready-mixed in large bags will also give good results.

You can use containers to plant either bare-root bushes or plants already growing in nursery cans. Roses that already have a head start growing in containers seem to adapt better to container gardening: Perhaps it's because their roots have already adjusted to a confined space. Bare-root plants, in contrast, come directly from fields.

If you choose a porous clay pot, soak it for about 30 minutes before you plant the rose, so the clay won't rob the roots of moisture. When you're ready to plant, place pieces of broken pottery or screen over the drainage holes to stop soil from washing through.

Add a few scoops of soil and set the plant at the correct height, just as you would if you were planting it in the ground. Keep adding soil, packing it down well to eliminate any air pockets. For easier watering, leave 1½ to 2 inches between the soil level and the top of

Growing Roses in Containers

1. Place broken crockery or screen over the drainage holes.

2. Add soil and set plant at correct height. Pour in more soil, leaving a watering space of 1½" to 2" at top of container.

3. Pack the soil well to eliminate air pockets, then soak thoroughly.

the pot. After you've filled the pot, soak the soil thoroughly.

You can cover the soil with a mulch, plant a shallow-rooted ground cover such as Scotchmoss or babytears, or add a few seedling annuals to dress up the container and provide color before the roses start to bloom.

Place the container where the plant will get at least six hours of direct morning and midday sunlight. If the bush starts to lean toward the sun, find a sunnier location and rotate the pot every few days to ensure that the plant grows evenly. Keep the plant away from light-colored walls during hot sunny days. Reflected heat can burn the foliage.

MINIATURE ROSES

Miniature roses enjoy the same soil and care as their larger relatives. Since they grow on their own roots (that is, they're not grafted), you don't have to worry about the position of a bud union when planting. But whether you are planting a miniature in a container or in the ground, set it slightly deeper than it originally grew.

To plant miniatures in the garden, dig holes 8 to 10 inches deep, and space them about 10 to 12 inches apart. You may want to space the plants further apart in a warm-winter area, where miniatures tend to grow more vigorously. Make sure the roses are not too close to large plants that might rob them of much-needed sunshine and moisture.

Remember that catalog descriptions of miniature plant sizes are usually based on indoor or greenhouse pot culture, where size is regulated by restricted root growth. Although the flowers will remain tiny, many of the miniature plants will grow 2½ to 3 feet tall and nearly as wide when planted in the ground, especially in warm climates. To keep the bushes small, you may have to prune them back severely every year.

To grow miniature roses in containers, choose pots 4 to 10 inches in diameter. If you will be growing them indoors, use a packaged synthetic soil mix instead of garden soil to prevent the spread of pests and diseases.

LABELING

Patented roses are sold with name tags attached by wire, which can cut into the cane as it grows. Remove the tag at planting time

Top left: Miniature roses grow more vigorously in the ground.
Top right: Set the plant slightly deeper in the hole than it was in the pot.
Center left: Tamp down the soil around the roots to eliminate any air pockets.
Center right: After planting, water thoroughly by filling the basin.
Bottom: Permanent labels identify each of these miniatures.

and attach it to a stake near the plant. You can, of course, fashion your own label in the style of your choice.

Sketch a diagram of the landscape and write in the names of the roses, planting dates, sources, and any other useful information. This may be valuable in years to come, especially to identify a rose whose label has been lost or to know the age of the plants.

An organic bark mulch around this planting of grandiflora 'Pink Parfait' helps retain soil moisture and reduces weeding.

Mulching Materials

Bark	Available commercially in chip form or finely ground. Very attractive and long lasting.
Sawdust, wood chips, or wood shavings	Low in plant nutrients; decomposes slowly; tends to pack down. Well-composted material preferred, although fresh wood products can be used. When used as a surface mulch, fresh wood doesn't deplete nitrogen supply as it does when worked into the soil. (Normal fertilizer program will take care of nitrogen requirements of uncomposted wood mulch.) Keep away from building foundations; may attract termites.
Grass clippings or hay	Probably the most readily available, but unattractive. Let dry before spreading. Repeated use builds up reserve of nutrients that lasts for years.
Gravel or stone chips	Not too attractive with roses. Extremely durable, holds down weeds, but does not supply nutrients or humus.
Mushroom compost	Often available in areas where commercial mushrooms are produced. Usually inexpensive, with a good color that blends into the landscape.
Newspaper	Readily available. Can be shredded or used as sheets, and held in place by rocks, bricks, or soil. Cover with more attractive material. Builds humus, and ink contains beneficial trace elements.
Pine needles	Will not mat down. Fairly durable. Potential fire hazard.
Rotted manure	High in salts, so make sure it is well rotted. May contain weed seeds if obtained from a farm or stable. Can be purchased heat-treated.
Straw	Long lasting. Depletes nitrogen when worked into the soil, but furnishes considerable potassium.
Tree leaves (whole or shredded)	Excellent source of humus. Rots rapidly; high in nutrients.
Landscape fabric	Excellent. Discourages weeds while allowing water to penetrate. Can be covered with thin layer of bark or other material for a more attractive appearance.

MULCHING

Mulching—spreading a protective covering on top of the soil—has many advantages for the rose gardener. In addition to giving a neat, attractive appearance to rose beds, it slows the evaporation of moisture from the soil and prevents the formation of a hard crust. Left in place all year, it insulates the soil, preventing rapid temperature changes in the soil during the winter as well as the summer.

Mulching is also invaluable in weed control. It is best not to cultivate to control weeds, as deep cultivation around roses—more than 1 to 1½ inches—will damage feeder roots.

Apply a mulch around the rose plants or over a whole bed. You can use either an organic mulch like bark, or an inorganic mulch like stone chips. Generally, rose gardeners use organic mulches; as the materials break down, they improve the soil.

Many rose gardeners are discovering the benefits of laying landscape fabric—an inorganic mulch—underneath a cover mulch like bark chips. A relatively recent development, landscape fabric resembles black plastic. However, it allows water through while blocking the light that weeds need for germination.

After planting, apply 2 to 4 inches of mulch. Do not let it mound up around the base of the plants. If you have had problems with fungus diseases, remove all the old mulch yearly in early fall and replace it with fresh mulch.

The accompanying chart lists the advantages and disadvantages of various mulching materials. There may also be other good choices available locally.

Watering Roses

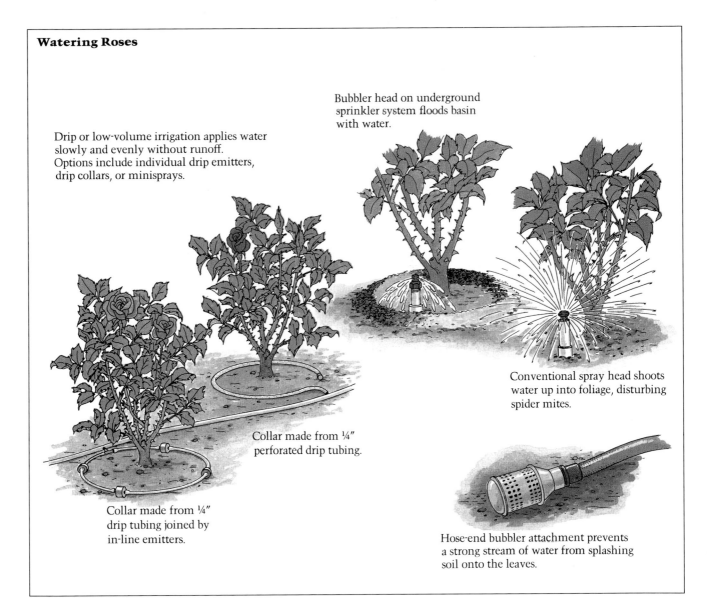

Drip or low-volume irrigation applies water slowly and evenly without runoff. Options include individual drip emitters, drip collars, or minisprays.

Bubbler head on underground sprinkler system floods basin with water.

Conventional spray head shoots water up into foliage, disturbing spider mites.

Collar made from ¼″ perforated drip tubing.

Collar made from ¼″ drip tubing joined by in-line emitters.

Hose-end bubbler attachment prevents a strong stream of water from splashing soil onto the leaves.

WATERING

One thing all rose gardeners agree on is that you can't give a rose too much water. Rose foliage will wilt if there is insufficient moisture, and during the growing season rose leaves should always be turgid. Moisture should be retained by the soil, and at the same time drainage should be excellent so that the roots are not standing in water. (See pages 37 and 38 for methods to correct poor soil drainage.)

Watering Roses in the Garden

It's difficult to prescribe how much or how often to water roses in the garden. The frequency of watering as well as the amount depend on soil type, climate, and the growth stage of the rose. More water is needed when the soil is loose and sandy, when the air is hot and dry, or when the roses are newly planted.

Be particularly attentive to a newly planted rose if spring is unusually warm or early. The root system may not have developed enough to provide sufficient moisture to the growing foliage, which is stimulated by the warmth of the sun.

Normally a rose should receive 1 to 2 inches of water per week, all at one time, starting in early spring and continuing through fall. Hot and dry weather may make it necessary to water every three or four days. Porous soils benefit from additional deep soakings.

There are several ways to water roses. The method you choose may depend on where you live, the size of your garden, the need to conserve water, and other factors. Many rose gardeners use drip irrigation; others prefer underground sprinklers; and still others water by hand.

The most efficient watering method is drip, or low-volume, irrigation, which applies water slowly without runoff. You can place one drip emitter on each side of a rosebush, use manufactured drip collars, or fashion your own collars with perforated drip tubing or tubing joined together with in-line emitters.

Some rose gardeners prefer conventional spray heads because the streams of water directed up onto the leaves disturb spider mites, which live on the undersides of leaves. Although low-volume minisprays apply water more economically, they don't do as good a job of getting water up into the foliage. If you are wetting the foliage, do it in the early morning so that the leaves will dry before evening.

Bubbler attachments on hoses are popular with gardeners who water by hand. Water floods into basins formed around the rosebushes and slowly soaks into the soil. The bubbler attachment prevents a strong stream from eroding the soil or splashing dirt or mulch on the foliage. (Some gardeners with underground sprinkler systems use bubbler heads to accomplish the same task more conveniently.)

Whichever method you use, be sure to water deeply, soaking the soil to a depth of 16 to 18 inches. A light sprinkling is worse than no water at all. Frequent light applications result in a shallow root system that will not physically support the plant and will require continued frequent waterings. Lightly watered plants are also more susceptible to injury from cultivation and to fertilizer burn.

If you're not sure how deep water is penetrating, apply water for a measured period of time and then dig down near the roots and measure the depth to which the soil is damp. If the soil is damp to a depth of only 8 inches, for example, you'll probably have to water about twice as long as you did.

Watering Roses in Containers

Ample watering is even more critical for container plants because they have much less soil from which to draw moisture. A rose that lacks moisture will be stunted, and if it goes without sufficient water often or for a long period, it will die. Check the amount of moisture deep in the pot at least every couple of days during the summer and every day when the weather is very hot or windy.

Wood, plastic, and glazed pottery containers lose less moisture to the surrounding air than do unglazed pots. Placing the container inside another will insulate it and reduce moisture loss. Be sure the outside container has drainage holes so that the roots are not standing in water.

FERTILIZING

Most roses need regular applications of fertilizer to reach their full size and produce abundant flowers. A healthy, well-fed plant is also better able to resist attacks of pests and diseases and to survive severe winter cold.

The rate and frequency of fertilizer application and the appropriate fertilizer to use depend on the type of garden soil. Plants in sandy soil need frequent applications; those in a heavy soil may not need as many. A soil test will help determine the particular balance of the three major nutrients—nitrogen, phosphorus, and potassium—that your garden needs. The staff of a local nursery can often recommend the fertilizer ratio and application rates for your area.

Kinds of Fertilizers

Both natural organic and synthetic fertilizers are available in dry or liquid preparations. Organic fertilizers, derived from plants and animals, act more slowly and need microorganisms to break them down into elements usable by roots. Synthetic fertilizers act on the plant more quickly; they must also be reapplied more frequently.

Dry fertilizers are worked into the ground and are spread to the roots by watering. Liquid fertilizers are added to water and usually applied to the roots. Foliar liquid fertilizers are sprayed onto the leaves, which absorb the nutrients.

Many rose gardeners rely on a complete (meaning that it contains nitrogen, phosphorus, and potassium) dry fertilizer and supplemental applications of a liquid fertilizer. Moisten the soil before you apply a fertilizer; water again after you've applied it to carry the nutrients to the roots. Do not spray fertilizer on foliage on hot (over 85° F) days. Whatever kind of fertilizer you use, always follow exactly the directions and the dosage recommendations on the product label. Excessive doses of fertilizer can severely harm a plant.

Frequency of Application

Species roses, old roses, and climbers usually need only one application of fertilizer in the early spring as the buds prepare to burst. *Remontant* (repeat-blooming) old roses and climbers will benefit from a second feeding of liquid fertilizer after the first bloom.

Modern roses need regular feeding to provide energy for growth and blooms. Begin fertilizing newly planted roses once they are established, about three to four weeks after planting. Start fertilizing older plants after they have been pruned and the new foliage starts to appear.

There are two schools of thought on the frequency of subsequent applications. Some gardeners favor applications of fertilizer every six to eight weeks, or three or four times, during the growing season. Other gardeners swear by applications every three to five weeks, usually alternating dry and liquid fertilizers in reduced amounts. Both recommendations are based on using synthetic, fast-release fertilizers. Fast-draining sandy soil benefits from the more frequent applications. You'll probably want to experiment and see which method works best for you.

In regions where winter temperatures drop below 10° F, stop applying fertilizers that contain nitrogen six weeks before the anticipated first frost, and apply instead a fertilizer containing only phosphorus and potassium to strengthen the plant for the winter.

Iron-Deficiency Chlorosis

Chlorosis is an unnatural yellowing of foliage. Iron deficiency causes interveinal chlorosis—the tissue between the veins turns yellow and the veins remain green. This condition is caused by a shortage of iron available to the plant as a result of poor drainage, excess lime in the soil, or a naturally alkaline soil. Preparing the planting site properly, using the results of a soil test, is the best prevention.

Roses with some yellow or orange shading in the petals are most susceptible to iron chlorosis. Spraying the leaves with a solution of chelated iron fertilizer will take care of mild cases. For severe cases, improve the soil by working in iron chelate fertilizer around the plant according to label directions; improve the drainage; or treat alkaline soil with agricultural sulfur as described on page 38.

Ingredients in a Balanced Plant Diet

Elements	Contributions	Signs of malnutrition
Primary elements		
Nitrogen	Green growth Used most heavily when plant is growing fastest	Yellow leaves No new growth Buds fail to open Small, pale flowers
Phosphorus	Good root growth and flower production	Dull green foliage Falling leaves Weak stems Abnormal root system Slow-to-open buds
Potassium	Vigorous growth	Leaf margins yellow and turn brown Weak stems Underdeveloped buds
Secondary elements		
Calcium	Growth of plant cells and good roots	Deformed growth and abnormal root development
Magnesium	Good growth	Mature yellow leaves tinged maroon
Sulfur	Green growth	New leaves turn yellow
Trace elements		
Boron	Good form	Small, curled, and scorched leaves Dead terminal buds
Chlorine	Good growth	Malformed foliage
Copper	Good growth	Poorly developed tips
Iron	Green growth	Yellow leaves with green veins
Manganese	Green growth	Pale mottling of leaves
Molybdenum	Good growth	Poorly developed leaves
Zinc	Good growth	Malformed growth

Fertilizing Roses in Containers

Because roses grown in containers are watered more often and nutrients are thus leached from the soil at a faster rate, these plants need more frequent applications of fertilizer. Whether you are using dry or liquid fertilizer, a good rule of thumb is to halve the recommended dosage and apply it twice as often as directed on the label. Again, don't overfertilize. If you mistakenly apply too much, give the plant several thorough soakings of water to wash the excess fertilizer out of the soil.

Control aphids with regular applications of a pesticide.

PESTS AND DISEASES

Take a leisurely walk through the garden every few days and enjoy the rewards of your labor. At the same time keep your eyes open for early signs of trouble, such as wilted foliage, deformed flower buds, or spots on leaves.

If you discover such warnings, don't jump to the conclusion that your garden is disease- or pest-ridden. Take time to diagnose the problem. If you find insects on the plants, for example, be sure they're not beneficial insects that prey on damaging insects. Remember, too, that many plant problems can be caused by a gardener's oversight or neglect. Not enough water causes wilt; too much water can cause rot; alkaline soil can cause yellow leaves. Before spraying, make sure the problem is not a cultural one. Symptoms, diagnoses, and methods of control of common insects and diseases attacking roses are listed in the chart on pages 50 and 51.

Prevention Is the Key

A healthy and vigorous rose can withstand more injury than a rose that is under stress from lack of water or nutrients.

Buy high-quality plants that show no abnormal swellings on the roots or crown (where the stem and the roots meet, just below the bud union) and no discolored areas on the canes. The bud union should be free of cracks. Buy from reliable sources that guarantee their products to be disease-free. To further reduce the chance of disease, choose one of the many cultivars that have proved particularly resistant to common rose diseases.

Some diseases can be prevented by watering correctly. If you are watering overhead, water only in the morning so the foliage has a chance to dry out before nightfall. If you are irrigating by hand, use a water bubbler on the end of the hose to prevent soil or mulch from splattering on the leaves. This technique slows the spread of certain diseases, such as blackspot.

Perform maintenance pruning throughout the growing season. Remove all canes showing cankers, or discolored sunken spots, as soon as you detect them, and destroy the prunings. Remove and destroy individual leaves bearing black spots as soon as you notice them.

Don't forget a winter cleanup. There will be fewer insects and disease organisms when the new leaves unfurl in the spring if you clean all debris from the beds when the roses are dormant. To keep rust and blackspot from carrying over from year to year, strip all leaves from the bushes, even in warm-winter areas where leaves may tend to remain on the plants. Rake up any leaves that have fallen, and burn them or dump them in the garbage can. Spray the plant and the soil or mulch with a dormant oil spray.

Establish a regular spray schedule for pest and disease control during the growing season. You may never see any evidence of pests or disease if you regularly take the time every two weeks or so to spray or dust the plants with a multipurpose pesticide. This program shouldn't take more than about an hour every two weeks for most rose plantings.

Systemics   A systemic is a pesticide that is absorbed into a plant's system, making the plant toxic to pests. Systemic insecticides come in two forms: a liquid concentrate applied as a spray, and dry granules that often contain nutrients as well as insecticide so that one application serves a number of purposes. If applied every six weeks, this kind of pesticide eliminates the need for routine spraying against aphids, spider mites, whiteflies, leaf miners, leafhoppers, and other sucking insects. The plant has internal protection that cannot be washed off by rain or by water from sprinklers.

Natural controls   Predaceous insects such as the ladybird beetle, praying mantis, Trichogramma wasp, and lacewing can help keep the population of aphids and certain other pests under control. If you use chemical sprays or dusts, you may kill these beneficial insects.

Birds can be a menace to the vegetable garden or fruit orchard, but they are a delightful asset to the rose garden. Insect-eating species include bluebirds, chickadees, mockingbirds, orioles, robins, wrens, and warblers. Welcome them by hanging bird feeders near the roses.

Using Chemical Controls

There may be times when you are faced with an invasion of pests overwhelming your usual methods of control. In such cases it's important to act quickly. Spray or dust at the very first sign of attack. Get the first aphids, the

Systemic Rose Care

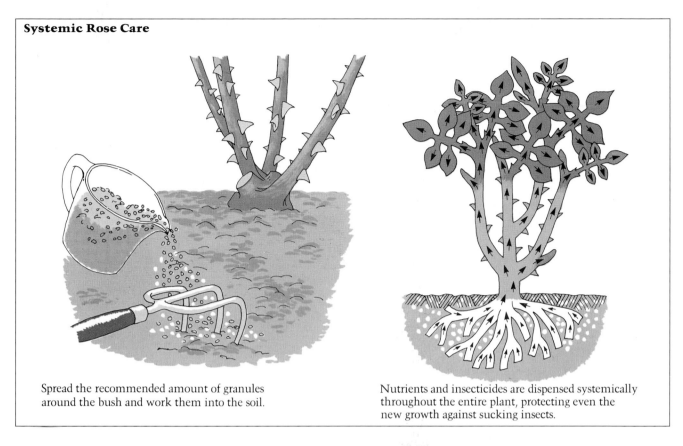

Spread the recommended amount of granules around the bush and work them into the soil.

Nutrients and insecticides are dispensed systemically throughout the entire plant, protecting even the new growth against sucking insects.

first brood of beetles, or the first invasion of thrips, and you'll be able to establish complete control much more quickly.

Use garden chemicals thoughtfully and carefully. Keep in mind the following guidelines for their safe, effective use.

☐ Store all chemicals behind locked doors, in their original containers with labels intact. Keep them away from food or drink and out of the reach of children and pets.

☐ Observe all directions and precautions on pesticide labels. They are there for your benefit and safety.

☐ Use pesticides at the correct dosage and intervals as specified on the label to avoid unnecessary residues and injury to plants and animals. Never use a stronger spray than is recommended by the manufacturer. The sprays have been carefully formulated by experts to do the most effective job.

☐ Water plants thoroughly the day before spraying.

☐ Mix chemicals in an open area. Spray on calm days to prevent drift. Work on the windward side when applying them. Cover any nearby fish ponds or birdbaths. Wear protective clothing when spraying, and avoid prolonged inhalation of any chemical.

☐ Spray or dust the tops and the undersides of the leaves. Insects and diseases often work on the lower surfaces of leaves.

☐ Always use up any sprays the same day you mix them. Do not store them for future use.

☐ Dispose of surplus pesticides and empty containers in such a way that you do not contaminate water or soil. Wrap them in paper and place them in the garbage can. If there are special rules for pesticide disposal in your area, abide by them.

☐ After handling pesticides, be sure to wash up before you eat, drink, or smoke.

Discourage blackspot by keeping the foliage dry and by cleaning up any debris.

Combating Pests and Diseases

Symptoms		Problems	Solutions
Clusters of tiny insects on young shoots, flower buds, or underside of leaves. Foliage and blooms stunted or deformed. Sticky honeydew attracts ants.	 Enlarged 2x	Aphids. Soft-bodied green, brown, or reddish insects that suck plant juices.	Harmless ladybird beetles introduced into the garden will feed on aphids. Wipe out infestations with contact sprays such as acephate (Isotox®, Orthene®, or Orthenex®), diazinon, or malathion.
Foliage, flowers, and stems are chewed, devoured, or have holes drilled in them.	 All life-size	Beetles (including 1. Japanese, 2. rose chafer, 3. rose curculio, and 4. Fuller beetles). Their larvae also eat plant roots.	Pick off beetles by hand or knock them into a can of kerosene and water. Spray with acephate (Isotox® or Orthene®), carbaryl (Sevin®), diazinon, or malathion.
Circular black spots with fringed margins appear on leaves. Leaves may turn yellow and drop prematurely. On more resistant varieties, leaves will remain green and hang onto bush.		Blackspot. A fungus disease, easily spread to nearby bushes by rain or hose. Overwinters in small cane lesions or leaves left on ground.	Water with wand or soil soaker. If you must wet foliage, do it early in the day so the bush dries before night. Spray regularly with triforine (Funginex® or Orthenex®) or chlorothalonil (Daconil 2787®).
Flower buds eaten or leaves rolled or tied around the pest and eaten from inside. Most often a late spring problem.	 Life-size	Budworm and other caterpillars. Larvae of moths and butterflies that feed on foliage.	Cut out infested buds and leaves. Apply acephate (Isotox® or Orthene®), carbaryl (Sevin®), or diazinon at first sign of damage.
Holes eaten into leaves from the underside, causing a skeletonized effect. Appear early in spring. Later large holes are eaten in leaves and finally the veins are devoured.	 Approx. life-size	Bristly rose slugs (often called cane borers or leafworms). Half-inch-long, hairy, slimy larvae of sawfly. Young eat underside of leaves; adults eat entire leaf.	Act quickly to stop the speedy damage. Spray with carbaryl (Sevin®) or acephate (Isotox® or Orthene®).
Lesions in the woody tissue of a cane, poor growth, or death above the affected area.		Canker. A disease caused by a parasitic fungus that usually enters plant through wounds or dying tissue.	Prune out and burn all affected tissue, cutting well below canker with shears dipped in alcohol after each cut. Apply pruning paint or sealer.
Roundish, rough-surfaced growths near plant crown or on roots. Plant loses vigor, produces abnormal flowers and foliage, and eventually dies.		Crown gall. Soil-borne bacterial disease that can live in soil after affected plant is removed and may or may not affect a new plant.	Do not buy plants with swellings near bud union or on roots. Remove and burn infected parts, seal with pruning paint. Or remove entire bush and treat soil with all-purpose fumigant such as Vapam® before setting out new plants.
Top surface of leaves turns pale and becomes covered with tiny yellow specks similar to damage of spider mites.	 Life-size Enlarged 3x	Leafhoppers. Tiny, greenish yellow, jumping insects found on underside of leaves. They suck out contents of leaf cells.	Apply acephate (Isotox®, Orthene®, or Orthenex®), diazinon, or malathion.
Pale green foliage and stunted growth in spite of good gardening practices. Root examination reveals abnormal swelling, knotty enlargements with tiny white eggs inside, discolored lesions, or dead tissue.	 Enlarged approx. 5x	Nematodes. Tiny animal pests that invade the roots of the plant.	Check with your Cooperative Extension Agent or Agricultural Experiment Station for help in diagnosis and control. All-purpose soil fumigant or nematocide such as Vapam® is beneficial.

Combating Pests and Diseases

Symptoms		Problems	Solutions
Holes in cut ends of canes or punctures in stems. Wilted plant shoots, foliage, and canes. Sometimes slight swelling of canes.	1. 2. 3.	Pithborers (including 1. rose stem sawfly, 2. rose stem girdler, and 3. small carpenter bee). Pests that bore into cane and lay eggs. Larvae eat through canes.	Cut canes below infested portion during spring pruning. Seal exposed tips with pruning paint.
White powdery masses of spores on young leaves, shoots, and buds; distorted young shoots; stunted foliage.		Powdery mildew. Disease spread by wind and rain. Encouraged by warm days followed by cool nights. Overwinters on fallen leaves and inside stems and bud scales.	Apply triforine (Funginex® or Orthenex®). For best results, apply when mildew is first noticed. Repeated applications required to give control.
Large mossy or callused swellings on stems or roots that look like crown gall, but if you cut them open you'll find larvae. (Mostly on species roses.)		Rose gall (including mossy rose gall and rose root gall). Wasplike insects that bore into canes and lay eggs. The growing larvae cause swelling.	Insecticides do not control. Prune and burn infested stems to destroy larvae before they emerge. Seal exposed area.
Black, deformed flower buds and leaves that die prematurely.	Enlarged 3x	Rose midge. Tiny yellowish flies that lay eggs in growing tips of stems. Hatching maggots destroy tender tissue.	Remove and destroy affected stem tips. Spray with acephate (Isotox® or Orthene®) at first sign of infestation. Timing is critical, as these insects breed extremely fast and can destroy all the blossoms on a rose plant overnight.
Wilted and dark foliage that drops prematurely. Close examination reveals mature stems encrusted with hard-shelled insects.	Approx. life-size	Rose scales. Round, dirty white, gray, or brown shell-covered insects that suck sap from plants.	Prune out and destroy old, infested wood. Apply acephate (Orthene®), carbaryl (Sevin®), dormant oil spray (Volck®), or malathion.
Wilted leaves that may drop. Yellow dots and light green mottling appear on upper leaf surface opposite pustules of powdery, rust-colored spores on the lower surface.		Rust. Disease spread by wind and rain. Overwinters on fallen leaves. Especially troublesome along the Pacific Coast.	Remove and destroy all affected leaves during pruning. Spray with triforine (Funginex® or Orthenex®). Select rust-resistant varieties for new plantings.
Stippled leaves appear dry, turn brown, red, yellow, or gray, then curl and drop off. Sometimes webs are visible on the underside of leaves.		Spider mites. Minute pests that suck juices from underside of foliage. Abundant in hot, dry weather.	Clean up trash and weeds in early spring to destroy breeding places. Spray infestations with diazinon, dormant oil spray (Volck®), hexakis (Isotox®, Orthenex®, or Vendex®), or malathion.
Flecked petals and deformed flowers, especially on white varieties.		Thrips. Very active, tiny, slender, brownish yellow, winged insects that hide in base of infected flowers.	Cut off and dispose of spent blooms. Apply acephate (Isotox®, Orthene®, or Orthenex®), diazinon, or malathion.
Small, angular, colorless spots on foliage. Ring, oak leaf, watermark, or mosaic pattern develops on leaves.		Virus diseases (including mosaic). Spread by propagating infected plants.	The only control is prevention. Do not buy any plants exhibiting the symptoms. Remove entire affected plant to prevent spread to nearby plants.

PROTECTION FROM THE ELEMENTS

Most roses are quite resilient plants ("glorified brambles," as one cranky rosarian observed), but many do need some protection from extreme fluctuations in temperature and the drying effects of wind. All roses will respond with their best flower display and prove a credit to your garden if you pamper them a little.

Wind

Any strong, constant wind is bad for roses. Wind hastens the evaporation of moisture from the leaves. In extreme cases, even if the soil is damp, the plant becomes severely dehydrated because it is unable to draw moisture from the roots fast enough to replenish the evaporated moisture. A hedge of more resilient shrubs or a fence will sometimes help shield the roses.

A hot and dry wind is particularly troublesome to roses. A fence will likely not be sufficient protection in this situation. Air on the leeward side of a fence that is built solid and has no openings is more turbulent than on the leeward side of a hedge. And, most important, a fence doesn't add moisture to dry air as a screen of shrubs or trees does.

Allow at least 10 feet between rosebushes and a screen or hedge. Select deep-rooted shrubs that grow well in your climate.

Heat

Very hot weather fatigues a rose plant. At temperatures above 90° F, the plant uses food faster than its foliage can manufacture it from sunlight, water, and nutrients. In a hot climate, be careful not to overprune roses. During the winter, prune only to shape the plants. Less-severe pruning allows a greater abundance of foliage to develop to provide the plant with a store of energy before the hot summer months. Rose gardeners in cooler climates need not be so restrained.

In extremely hot, sunny areas you might erect a lath covering over the roses to give some shade during the hottest part of the day. Roses in containers should be moved to partially shaded locations.

Cool nights or dark, damp days can cause balling—blooms open halfway and then stop. If you cut off such blooms when they start to ball, the plant will grow better when weather conditions improve. In a cool or foggy summer area, you might select rose varieties with fewer petals, which are less prone to balling.

Sometimes, after very mild or warm winters, branch tips will remain bare or the side buds on some canes will fail to grow; this is because they were not chilled enough to induce normal growth. Prune out such canes, since they will not recover and grow normally.

Freezing

The question of protecting roses from freezing is probably the most controversial matter in rose culture. Some experts go so far as to advise against any winter protection for roses except a deep layer of mulch, even in very harsh climates. On the other side are people in the same area who recommend tipping and burying the entire plant. Talk with neighbors or friends or members of your local rose society to find out which methods provide sufficient protection in your area.

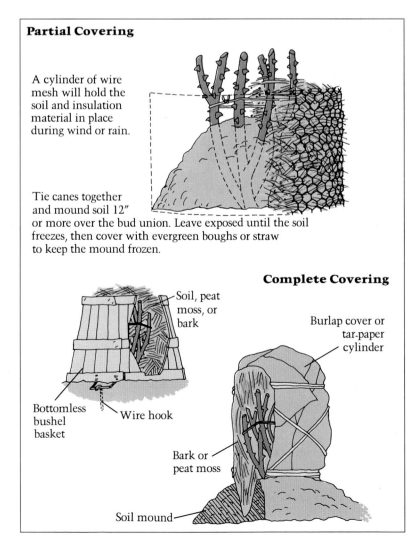

Partial Covering

A cylinder of wire mesh will hold the soil and insulation material in place during wind or rain.

Tie canes together and mound soil 12" or more over the bud union. Leave exposed until the soil freezes, then cover with evergreen boughs or straw to keep the mound frozen.

Complete Covering

Soil, peat moss, or bark

Burlap cover or tar-paper cylinder

Bottomless bushel basket

Wire hook

Bark or peat moss

Soil mound

Plants that can withstand freezing temperatures are called hardy; those unable to tolerate such cold are referred to as tender. There are degrees of hardiness. Quite a few species roses, shrub roses, old roses, and climbers naturally withstand freezing temperatures and need little or no protection. A number of newer hybrid teas are marketed as subzero plants needing only minimal protection. Miniature roses are more cold-resistant than most hybrid teas or other garden roses and require little winter protection. In warm climates they even continue blooming all year.

One of a plant's best defenses against cold weather is proper summer care: Healthy, vigorous bushes are able to withstand cold far better than unhealthy ones. Also, roses planted in locations that are protected by trees, large shrubs, or structures fare better than bushes exposed to the elements.

Sudden changes in temperature in the fall, before the plant has hardened off for winter, can be disastrous. Early freezes kill more canes than much colder winter freezes. To discourage new growth that might be destroyed by an early freeze, avoid late-summer applications of nitrogen and hold back on watering.

In areas where temperatures drop to 10° to 15° F for as long as two weeks at a time, you can adequately protect most bush roses by mounding the base of each plant with fresh, loose soil or compost that drains well. After the first hard frost, mound up the soil to a height of 6 to 8 inches around the plants. Use soil from another area of the garden for mounding to avoid disturbing the roots. Prune each plant only enough to prevent the plant from whipping about in the wind or to fit it under a protective covering. Dispose of the clippings. Spray the plant with an anti-desiccant dormant spray; then spread 8 to 10 inches of leaves, straw, or other organic mulch around the plants and secure it with chicken wire or other netting.

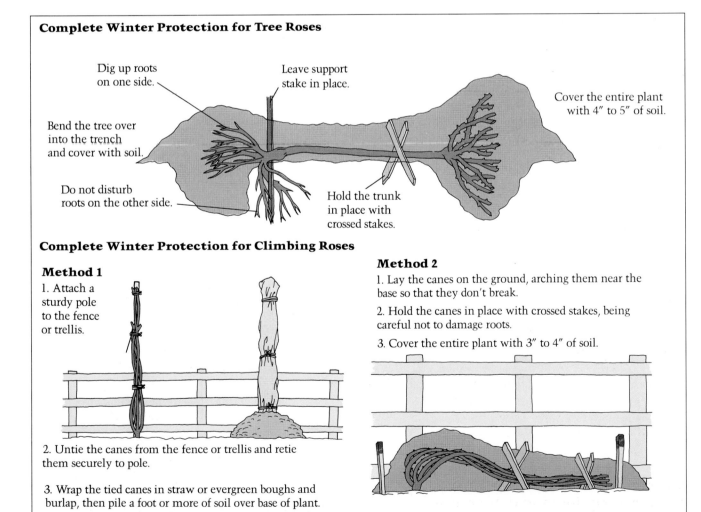

Complete Winter Protection for Tree Roses

Dig up roots on one side.

Leave support stake in place.

Cover the entire plant with 4″ to 5″ of soil.

Bend the tree over into the trench and cover with soil.

Do not disturb roots on the other side.

Hold the trunk in place with crossed stakes.

Complete Winter Protection for Climbing Roses

Method 1

1. Attach a sturdy pole to the fence or trellis.

2. Untie the canes from the fence or trellis and retie them securely to pole.

3. Wrap the tied canes in straw or evergreen boughs and burlap, then pile a foot or more of soil over base of plant.

Method 2

1. Lay the canes on the ground, arching them near the base so that they don't break.

2. Hold the canes in place with crossed stakes, being careful not to damage roots.

3. Cover the entire plant with 3″ to 4″ of soil.

Protective coverings called rose caps are available from garden suppliers, but you might like to devise your own from the examples illustrated on page 52. Prune the plants to fit under whatever cover you use; they may look scrawny the following spring, but they will regain their form by summer.

Where temperatures dip below zero, additional protection, such as completely burying the plant under soil, may be required.

Try not to be too eager to remove the protective coverings in the spring. The tender growth underneath can be killed by even a light frost. Keep some straw or mulch on hand to cover plants in the event of a late frost warning.

Roses in containers   When the temperature falls below 28° F, place roses growing in containers in an unheated shelter away from chilling winds. Even in the shelter the temperature should not fall below 10° F. When the bush begins to defoliate, remove all the leaves. Water occasionally during dormancy so the soil doesn't dry out completely. Do not feed. After the danger of frost is over, move the pot back outside. Prune the rose lightly to initiate new growth (see at right).

In mild areas where the temperature stays above 28° F, roses in containers can live outdoors all year. Cut back the water and eliminate feeding during the winter months to induce dormancy.

Tree roses   In warm-winter areas tree roses need no protection. In areas where winter temperatures remain above 28° F, wrap the plants in straw and cover them with burlap. If winter temperatures fall as low as 10° F, in late fall dig under the roots on one side until the plant can be pulled over on the ground without breaking any roots. Pin the plant to the ground and cover it entirely with 4 to 5 inches of soil. In spring, after the soil thaws and the danger of frost has passed, remove the soil and set the plant upright once again.

Climbing roses   There is no need to protect climbers in warm-winter areas. A burlap wrapping is adequate protection for climbing roses in mild climates. In areas with hard frosts, bury climbers the same way you do tree roses (see above).

PRUNING

A rose left unpruned can grow into a mass of tangled brambles that produce small or inferior blooms. Proper pruning removes unproductive or damaged wood and leaves a few good canes as the foundation for a healthy bush that will produce well-formed flowers. Pruning also allows you to create an attractive shape and to keep the rose to a size that fits the landscape.

Timing
Prune modern roses just before the plant breaks dormancy after the last frost. This can be anytime between January in warm areas and April in severe-winter climates.

Most old roses bear their flowers on wood produced the previous year, so they should be pruned only after they have bloomed.

Equipment
As an act of kindness both to your plants and to yourself, use sharp, clean, well-lubricated tools for pruning. For all roses except miniatures, you'll need three types of cutting instruments: hand pruning shears, long-handled lopping shears for thick canes and for hard-to-reach places, and a fine-toothed curved saw for cutting woody canes. Wear heavy-duty garden gloves when you prune.

To prune miniature roses, you'll need only a pair of hand pruners for thick stems and a smaller, more delicate pair of shears for trimming.

Making Cuts
Cut at sharp, 30- to 45-degree angles. Make any cuts to the base of the cane above the bud union, just above one of two forking branches, or to a strong outside bud or bud eye. A bud eye is a small bulge with a tiny "eye" and a horizontal crease below. At the end of the dormant period or when they are stimulated by pruning, bud eyes develop into new shoots.

Notice the direction in which the bud or bud eye is pointing. Prune to encourage outward-facing buds so that you do not end up with a tangle of canes competing for sunlight in the center of the bush. Make cuts about ¼ inch above the bud. If your cut is too high, you will leave a stub above the bud where the wood will die, providing a haven for pests and diseases.

Angle to Cut

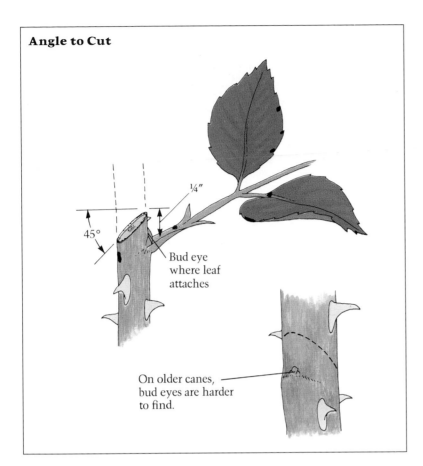

45°

¼"

Bud eye
where leaf
attaches

On older canes,
bud eyes are harder
to find.

When using pruning shears, ensure a clean cut by positioning the cutting blade on the side closer to the bud or the part of the cane that will remain on the plant. The slight injury that results from pressure on the noncutting side should be on the part of the cane that you discard.

How Much to Prune
Whatever kind of rose you're pruning, always cut away deadwood first. It's not going to come back to life, it's unattractive, and it harbors diseases. You can then make intelligent decisions about shaping the plant.

Pruning while the plant is dormant removes buds without reducing the energy stored in the roots and branches. The heavier the pruning, the more buds are removed, and the more energy will be available to each remaining bud.

About all that gardeners in severe climates need to do is cut back wood that has been killed during the winter. For those in more moderate or warm climates, there are three basic types of pruning. All three methods will be used by different gardeners within the same climatic zone. It usually takes several

years to learn the best pruning method for each variety of rose. You may discover that a light pruning works best, with a heavy pruning every four or five years. If you cut back too far one year, you'll know to go easier the next year.

Severe, or heavy The plant is cut back to three or four canes 6 to 10 inches high. This method is used to produce fewer but showier blooms for cut roses. It is also used to stimulate vigorous growth of weak plants. (Strongly growing plants don't need this treatment, because they can handle more buds and still grow vigorously.)

Moderate Five to twelve canes are left, about 18 to 24 inches high. Moderate pruning develops a much larger bush than severe pruning and is a better choice for most garden roses. The result of moderate pruning is smaller but numerous flowers.

Light Less than one third of the plant is cut back. Light pruning produces a profusion of short-stemmed flowers on larger bushes. This method is practiced mainly with floribundas, grandifloras, first-year hybrid teas, and species roses.

Pruning Bush Roses
It is easier to prune bush roses if the bud union is above ground. If it is below soil level, you may wish to remove soil from around the bud union while you are pruning so you can see the origin of all the canes.

First remove any deadwood down to the nearest healthy, dormant bud eye. Make the cut at least 1 inch below the dead area. If no live buds remain, remove the entire branch or cane to the bud union.

Examine the plant carefully for canker and other diseases (see pages 50 and 51). Cut canes to a plump bud at least 1 inch below any evidence of disease. Although the canes may look green and healthy, check the top of each one to make sure the pith in the center is creamy white, not brown or gray. Prune to the bud union if the pith is diseased all the way down.

Cut out weak, spindly, and deformed growth, including canes that grow straight out, then curve upward (called doglegs). Remove canes growing toward the center of the

Left: Pruning will rejuvenate this overgrown rosebush. Right: To open up a bush, remove the old canes with lopping shears.

Left: Use sharp hand-pruners to cut small canes and twigs. Right: A pruning saw makes removing woody growth simple.

Left: Severe pruning produces fewer but showier flowers. Right: Moderate pruning—nine canes are left here—produces a larger bush and more flowers.

bush. If two branches cross, remove the weaker one. Remove old canes at their base. Thick and woody, they produce a profusion of twigs rather than strong stems.

Remove all suckers, or reversion growth (undesired shoots that come from the rootstock below the bud union). You will notice that sucker foliage is different in color and form from the rest of the foliage. When removing this growth, cut as close to the base of the plant as you can, and even cut into the base if necessary. If you do not remove suckers, they will soon dominate the bush.

Next, thin out the remaining healthy canes to the shape you want and cut them back to the height you want. After severe winters, all the canes may have to be cut to within several inches of the bud union. In such cases you can't worry about shape; just save as much live wood as possible.

Pruning and Training Climbing Roses

Don't prune any climbers, except to cut out deadwood, for the first two or three years. This will allow them to establish mature canes. Climbers that bloom only once should be pruned after they have bloomed; climbing hybrid teas and other repeat-blooming climbers are pruned in early spring while they are dormant.

Prune ramblers and other once-blooming climbers soon after they flower. Cut out diseased or dead canes and remove older, gray canes as well as weak new ones; most climber canes are good for only two or three seasons. Save the green, healthy canes. Cut back the laterals, on which the flowers appear, to four or five sets of leaves to shape the plant the way you want it. Be sure to remove any suckers from the base of the plant.

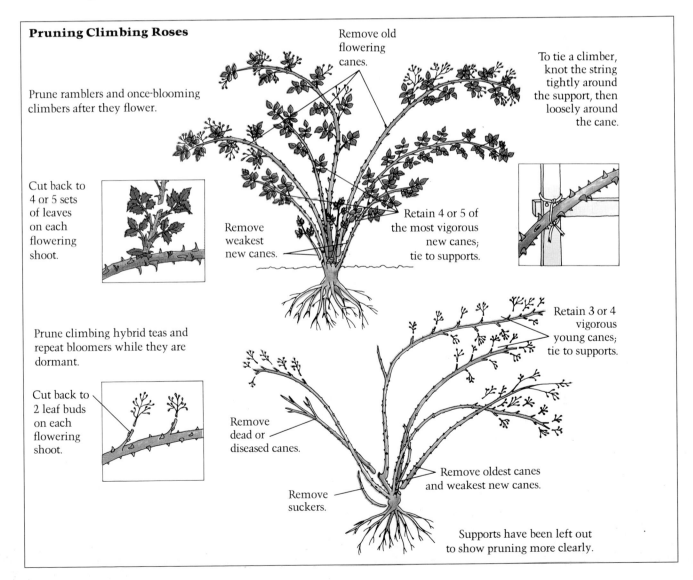

Pruning Climbing Roses

Prune ramblers and once-blooming climbers after they flower.

Cut back to 4 or 5 sets of leaves on each flowering shoot.

Prune climbing hybrid teas and repeat bloomers while they are dormant.

Cut back to 2 leaf buds on each flowering shoot.

Remove old flowering canes.

To tie a climber, knot the string tightly around the support, then loosely around the cane.

Remove weakest new canes.

Retain 4 or 5 of the most vigorous new canes; tie to supports.

Retain 3 or 4 vigorous young canes; tie to supports.

Remove dead or diseased canes.

Remove suckers.

Remove oldest canes and weakest new canes.

Supports have been left out to show pruning more clearly.

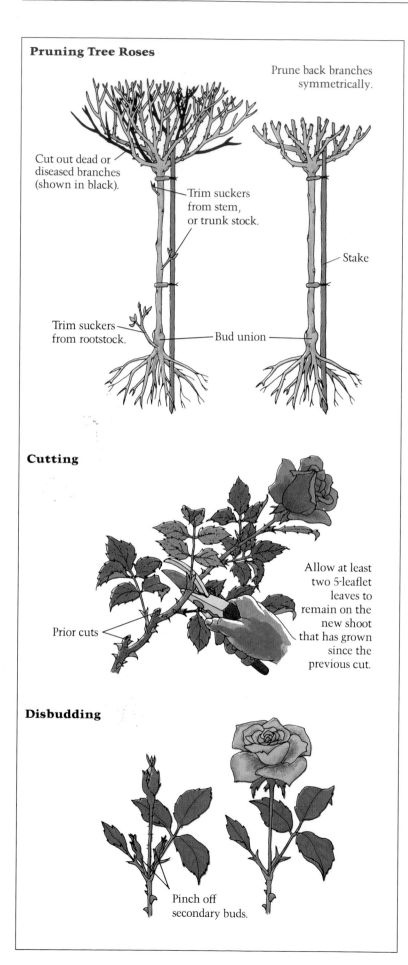

Pruning Tree Roses

Prune back branches symmetrically.

Cut out dead or diseased branches (shown in black).

Trim suckers from stem, or trunk stock.

Stake

Trim suckers from rootstock.

Bud union

Cutting

Prior cuts

Allow at least two 5-leaflet leaves to remain on the new shoot that has grown since the previous cut.

Disbudding

Pinch off secondary buds.

You'll need to trim some of the less vigorous climbers in spring to remove winterkill and twiggy growth. Later, after blooming is over, remove the faded flowers.

Prune climbing hybrid teas and everblooming large-flowered climbers while they are dormant. Do not take as much wood from the everbloomers as you do from the climbing hybrid teas. Proceed as you would with bush roses: Remove dead and diseased canes; get rid of suckers; and remove old or weak new growth. Retain three or four vigorous young canes. Cut back the laterals, on which the flowers appear, to two leaf buds.

Pluck the faded blossoms off everblooming climbers, but be careful not to take any foliage; the repeat blooms grow from the leaves immediately under the old flower cluster. When removing blooms from climbing hybrid teas, leave two sets of leaves on each flowering shoot.

Train climbers on arbors, fences, pergolas, pillars, or trellises by letting the canes grow long and then arching or tying them in a horizontal position with the tips of the canes pointed downward. This will stimulate the lateral buds to produce a flowering branch instead of concentrating growth in the terminal bud. (The illustration on page 57 shows how to tie the canes.) Shortening some of the long upright canes will stimulate the growth of laterals, which will help to cover the support.

Ramblers and other climbers can be pegged down, or their tips anchored to the ground, to produce sprawling plants.

Pruning Tree Roses

Prune standards in the same way as bush roses: Cut out dead or diseased canes, and prune back healthy canes to a good bud or bud eye. Keep the shape as symmetrical as possible so the foliage will fill out full and round. Remove any suckers from the rootstock or from the trunk stock, cutting as close to the base as possible.

Pruning Species and Shrub Roses

Most species and shrub roses need only a light trimming to shape them and to remove deadwood; their natural growth habit is part of their charm. Prune once-blooming roses after they bloom; prune repeat bloomers in winter or early spring.

Pruning Old Garden Roses

Old roses also should be pruned lightly. Prune one-time bloomers after flowering and repeat bloomers in winter or early spring.

Gallica   Remove twiggy growth after the flowers bloom. Shape lightly during the winter if desired.

Damask   Remove twiggy growth after flowering; cut back the lateral shoots to three sets of leaves. Cut back main canes to increase bushiness if desired.

Alba   Remove twiggy growth and cut back recent growth by one third after flowering.

Centifolia and moss   Reduce the canes and the side shoots by one third after blooming to produce a bushier plant.

China   Prune lightly by cutting back the side shoots about one third during the winter.

Bourbon and Portland   In winter cut back the main canes by one third and the side shoots to three buds. Trim twiggy growth after blooming.

Tea   Prune lightly as you would a hybrid tea rosebush.

Noisette   Prune bush forms as you would a hybrid tea. Prune climbing forms as you would a repeat-blooming climber.

Hybrid perpetual   After the plants bloom, cut back the main shoots by one third and shorten the side shoots.

Pruning Miniature Roses

Prune a miniature as you would a bush rose, but lightly. Very vigorous varieties grown outdoors in warm climates may need heavier pruning to maintain their compactness. Some of the very small miniatures, sometimes called micro-minis, may not need pruning at all.

Year-Round Care

Prune and groom roses as they grow. Cut out weak and spindly shoots, suckers, and obvious signs of disease. Remove flowers as soon as they have passed their peak.

Hybrid teas produce flowers in waves. Allowing the plant to set seeds delays the next blooming period. During the first growing season of a newly planted rose, snip off just the fading flowers, not any leaves; a young plant needs all the leaves it can produce. During subsequent growing seasons, don't snip off just the faded flowers. Instead, cut back the flowering stem to a five-leaflet leaf to encourage stronger growth. In cold-winter areas, allow hips to form after the final wave of flowers. The production of hips slows growth and prepares the plant for winter.

Rosarians who want to produce large blooms for shows disbud, or thin out flower buds, to improve the quality of bloom. They pinch off all but a selected few terminal buds.

PROPAGATION

Starting new roses from existing plants is fairly easy. Duplicating roses that you already grow saves money, and it's fascinating to watch the new plants emerge and develop. You can exchange cuttings or seedlings with friends or other rosarians to build a collection of hard-to-find roses. Just be sure that the plants you reproduce are nonpatented roses (see page 20).

Sexual Reproduction

When you grow a rose from seed, you are propagating it sexually. Species roses can be duplicated from self-fertilized seeds. Other roses do not grow true from their own seeds; however, you can hybridize, or interbreed, plants to create a new rose that combines the characteristics of its parents. You can approach this scientifically with a certain rose in mind, or you can see what you come up with by rolling the genetic dice.

Hybridizing   All roses are bisexual. Nature has provided each rose with both stamens (male organs) and pistils (female organs) for pollination. Roses are hybridized by taking the pollen from the stamens on the flower of one cultivar and applying it to the pistils on the flower of another. The plants that are grown from the seeds of this cross will be the offspring of these two plants. The process begins early in the growing season to allow plenty of time for fertilization and seed production before dormancy sets in.

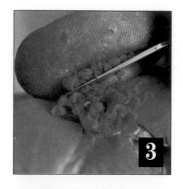

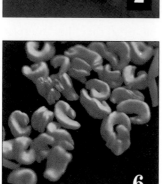

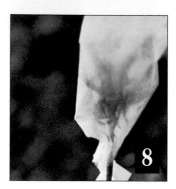

1. Remove the outer petals of the selected parent roses to expose the reproductive organs. 2. Pollen-bearing anthers are at the tips of the stamens, which surround the pistils in the center. 3. Remove the anthers from both parents before they self-pollinate the rose. 4. Store the anthers from the selected male parent inside a labeled container and allow them to dry. 5. A sticky secretion on the tips of the stigmas indicates that the female is pollen-receptive. 6. At about the same time, the anthers release dustlike pollen grains containing sperm. 7. Use a small, soft brush to place the dried pollen on the female stigmas. 8. Label the pollinated bud and protect it from dust and unwanted pollen by tying a bag over it.

Whether a plant serves as the male or as the female parent appears to have no effect on its ability to pass on its characteristics to the offspring. Breeders usually make reciprocal crossings, using the same variety as both a male and a female parent.

Early in the year, choose the cultivars you wish to pollinate. Then select a blossom on each plant that is less than half open. Leaving the flowers on the plants, carefully remove the petals from both flowers, and you will find both sets of reproductive organs. The very center contains the pistils—delicate stalks connected to an ovary at the base and a pollen-receiving stigma at the tip. Surrounding the pistils are the stamens—slender stalks tipped with anthers (sacs holding the pollen).

The first step in hybridization is to emasculate both parents. Even if you are using the rose as a female, you must remove the anthers before they have a chance to open and self-pollinate the rose. Pluck off the anthers with tweezers or cut them off with a sharp knife, being careful not to damage the pistils.

Choose the plant that will be the male parent and place the anthers from one of its flowers in a closed jar to dry; record the date and the cultivar on a label. (You can cut off and discard the flower from which you removed the anthers, or use it as a female in another experiment.) Cover the flower that you have chosen to be the female parent with a bag so that it cannot be fertilized by pollen that is carried by the wind.

During the next day or so, the anthers inside the jar will ripen and open, releasing their pollen grains—minute capsules that contain the sperm. During the same time, the female parent prepares to receive the pollen. When the female's stigmas are tipped with a sticky secretion, it is time for pollination.

Brush all the dry pollen onto the receptive stigmas with an artist's camel-hair brush. The secretion from the stigma not only makes the pollen adhere but also dissolves the capsules, releasing the tiny sperm. Once released, the sperm send tiny, hairlike pollen tubes down through the stalks to an ovule containing unfertilized eggs. There, a male reproductive cell seeks out and unites with an egg.

After the crossing is complete, label the female parent and identify the cultivar that served as the male parent. Tie the bag over the flower again to protect it from dust or unwanted pollen. Now it's up to nature. Don't be disappointed by a failure. The percentage of fertilizations is low.

The hip will dry up and fall off the plant if the pollination fails. If the pollination succeeds, the hip will stay green and swell with growth within a few weeks. Hips ripen in about two and a half months, turning bright

orange, yellow, red, or brown, depending on the cultivar. Gather the hip, along with the label, when it first turns color, before it becomes overripe. Fresh seeds germinate faster.

Slice the hip carefully with a knife, expose the seeds, and remove them. There may be only a single seed or as many as 50. Condition the seeds by storing them in plastic bags of peat moss. Refrigerate them at 40° F for about six weeks. When you remove the seeds from the refrigerator, plant them as outlined in the section that follows.

The first flowers may appear seven to eight weeks after germination. This will be your first glimpse of the results. Now you must make the decision, according to your personal preference, whether to continue growing the seedling or whether to discard it.

If you keep the seedling, you can either let it grow on its own roots or bud it onto a vigorous rootstock (see next page).

Growing from seed   Don't expect to produce a rose identical to a hybrid from its own seeds. Even if the plant self-pollinates, the seeds will not be true; the offspring will revert to some combination of its parents' characteristics.

Seed propagation can be used with self-pollinating species roses or with the seeds that result from hybridizing, or interbreeding two roses, as explained above.

Fill a shallow tray or flat with fine sand or vermiculite. Remove the seeds from the hip and plant them ½ inch deep. Water thoroughly. Keep the growing medium moist, not soggy, and warm (around 55° to 60° F). Withhold light for the first month; then give the tray 16 hours of light a day.

Germination soon begins, and it continues for two or three months. Seedlings emerge with a bent neck but straighten out in a few days. When the cotyledons, or seed leaves, stretch out horizontally and turn green, the seedlings are ready to be transplanted. The American Rose Society recommends a potting mix composed of equal parts of sterilized topsoil, perlite, and peat moss. To each quart of the mixture, add 1 ounce of dolomitic lime, 1 ounce of superphosphate, 1 ounce of rose food, and 1 ounce of 50 percent captan fungicide.

Transplant the seedlings into large, well-draining plastic or metal pans or flats. Give them 16 hours of good light per day in a warm place (70° F). Fluorescent fixtures provide excellent light for growing the seedlings.

Water sparingly and blot any water that remains on the leaves. Give the seedlings plenty of air circulation. After the first true leaves form, you may want to transplant the seedlings into 3-inch pots using the same soil mixture or to transplant them into the garden. Seedlings bloom when they are around two months old.

9. If the pollination is successful, the hip swells with growth (left). 10. Seeds, sometimes borne on the outside of the hip, can be harvested about two and a half months after the cross. 11. After the hip has matured and turned color, cut it carefully with a small, sharp knife. 12. To reveal the seeds, divide the hip into sections and peel them open. 13. Stratify seeds by storing them in peat moss at 40° F for up to six weeks. 14. Sow the seeds in a loose growing medium and allow them to germinate. This seedling is one week old. 15. Evaluate the results in about two months; weed out any weak or poorly colored seedlings. 16. Label promising seedlings for budding at the end of summer.

Vegetative Reproduction

Since hybrid roses do not reproduce true from seed, they must be propagated vegetatively, or asexually. A rose that is propagated from a cutting or by budding will be identical to the plant from which the cutting or bud was taken.

Hardwood cuttings   Use hardwood cuttings to propagate old garden roses and climbing roses. In late fall or early winter, cut pencil-diameter wood from the current season's growth into 5- to 6-inch lengths. Bury them vertically (in the same direction they were growing on the plant) in a box of sand or peat moss and store them in a cool, dark place (32° to 50° F). Keep the sand or peat moss moist through the winter. The plants should be ready to plant in the garden in spring.

If you live in a warm-winter climate, it may be difficult for you to find a place cool enough to store your cuttings. Look no further than your refrigerator. Wrap the cuttings in plastic and leave them in the refrigerator for two or three weeks. Then pot them (again, making sure they point in the same direction as they did on the plant) in sand and perlite, in peat moss, or in a synthetic soil; put the pot inside a plastic bag; and place the bag in the refrigerator for two or three months. Then remove the bag, place the pot in filtered sunlight, and begin watering.

Softwood cuttings   This is an easy way to reproduce favorite old garden roses and shrub roses. Cut 6- to 8-inch lengths of wood after the blooms have faded. Remove any flowers and the top few inches of each cutting. Remove the lower leaves, so that only one or two leaves remain at the top of the cutting. Dip the bottom of the cutting into a root hormone stimulant to speed up root development.

Set half the length of each cutting into a damp growing medium composed of equal parts of sand (or perlite) and peat moss (or vermiculite). Insert two tall stakes into the pot to support a plastic bag. Place the pot in the bag and seal it to create a greenhouse climate. Store the cuttings in a bright place away from direct sunlight. Remove the bag when new growth begins, usually after five to eight weeks. Transplant the cuttings to a container or a spot in the garden where they will be partially shaded for a couple of weeks.

Budding   Modern hybrid roses do not grow well on their own roots, so budding is the best way to propagate them.

In the fall or winter, select a healthy piece of rootstock. A sucker growing from below the bud union of an established plant is ideal root-stalk material. *Rosa multiflora* and 'Dr. Huey' are most commonly used for rootstocks,

Making Softwood Cuttings

Let the top two 5-leaflet leaves remain; pull off the lower leaves, being careful not to damage buds. Dip in root hormone stimulant.

Set the cuttings into damp soil mix.

Seal in a plastic bag until new shoots appear—about 5 to 8 weeks.

but any sturdy shrub or old rose that roots easily will do. Take 8- to 10-inch cuttings and root them individually in 10-inch pots, removing all but the top two buds.

The following spring or summer, cut a piece of budwood from the rose plant you wish to propagate, choosing a section 6 to 8 inches long from a stem that has just finished blooming. Using a small, sharp knife, cut a scion (a single bud and a small portion of the surrounding bark) from the budwood. On the rooted stock, just above the soil, make a shallow T-shaped cut in the outer tissue and insert the scion into the cut. Be sure that the bud is tucked all the way into the cut.

Bind the bud to the rootstock with a budding rubber or plastic gardening tape. The bud will develop in a few weeks; remove the binding when it does. Late in the following winter, cut off the rootstock just above the bud and let the new plant grow from the bud. Move the plant into the ground in the fall.

GROWING MINIATURE ROSES INDOORS

Miniature roses will bloom indoors all year, except for a resting period of about two months. You can expect a cycle of blooms every six to eight weeks. If you pot roses at various times, you will have a continuous flowering display. Select low-growing, compact varieties for indoors.

Plant a miniature rose in a 4- to 8-inch pot with a mixture of equal parts of sterilized garden soil, peat moss (or other humus-rich organic material), and coarse sand (or perlite). Be sure the container has excellent drainage. Soak the freshly planted rose in water up to the rim of the pot until the bubbling stops.

After planting and soaking the rose, put it on a cool porch, in a cold frame, or in a cool, protected outdoor area where it can acclimate itself for two to four weeks. When the plant begins to grow, bring it indoors and place it in a sunny window.

Keep the soil evenly moist, but never soggy. Occasionally let the surface dry, then water well from the top of the pot. Yellow leaves indicate inadequate drainage or too much water.

Yellow leaves may also be an indication that the surrounding air is too dry. Miniature roses like more moisture than the average house provides. You can increase humidity by placing the plant on a tray filled with pebbles or sand. Keep some water in the bottom of the tray but not enough to reach the underside of the pot. Washing the foliage routinely in the sink will help add moisture, remove any residues from sprays or household grease, and keep insects under control.

Feed indoor roses monthly and follow a preventive spray program to control diseases and pests, as you would for outdoor roses. (See page 48.) The worst enemy of miniature roses is the spider mite.

Some growers of miniature roses suggest an annual eight-week rest for plants during the hottest summer months. If possible, place the plant in the vegetable crisper of the refrigerator. After the forced dormancy, cut the plant back to one half its size and resume normal care. Alternatively, give the minis a fall rest by leaving them outside for a couple of months and bringing them inside again by the middle of December. Protect them from frost by placing them along a wall outside a heated room and covering them with straw. Prune the plants before bringing them back inside.

The plant should also be pruned anytime it is growing beyond the desired shape and size. Cut back about one third its height with sharp, clean shears to just above a five-leaflet leaf. Pinch new shoots to encourage branching. Remove spent blooms. You may need to repot yearly as you do for other indoor plants.

Using Artificial Light
Miniature roses are good candidates for light gardening. The plants remain compact, since they never have to reach for a light source, and they bloom profusely most of the year in cycles of six to eight weeks.

Place the plants under a light fixture that will provide 20 watts of light per square foot. Keep the light source 10 to 12 inches above the roses. Set the light fixture on a timer so that the plants get a routine 16 to 18 hours of light per day.

You can choose from a wide variety of lighting fixtures and bulbs. Many people favor the old reliable formula of equal light from fluorescent tubes and incandescent bulbs. You may choose two cool-white fluorescent tubes, one cool and one warm tube, or the full-spectrum fluorescents, such as Agrolite, Vitelite, or Durolite, which are designed for plant growth.

Enjoying Roses Indoors

Beautiful roses shouldn't be confined to the garden. Cut them to brighten any decor with color and fragrance, or preserve your roses in a potpourri.

T he charm, beauty, and fragrance of roses need not be confined to the garden—or to the growing season. Roses, both fresh-cut and preserved, have a place in the home throughout the year.

When roses are in bloom, bring the flowers indoors to brighten a dim corner of a room or to serve as a centerpiece for a party table setting. Be sure to pick rose varieties that will fill the room with a welcoming scent.

Even when the garden is slumbering, you can keep the memory of summer alive with roses preserved in various ways. Dry entire bouquets of your most exquisite roses to add cheer to your house and lift your spirits in winter. At the end of the growing season, collect the colorful seed capsules, or hips, and dry them for decoration. Dried flowers and hips also make wonderful gifts that can be given anytime of the year. Preserve the evocative scent of roses in cosmetic rose oil and in potpourri, an aromatic mixture of flower petals, herbs, and spices. You can even cook with roses: The petals lend delicate flavors to desserts, and the hips can be made into jams rich in vitamin C.

Miniature blooms, including 'Cinderella', 'Mary Marshall', 'Starina', and 'Over the Rainbow', are arranged casually in vases and jars.

Roses add a dainty touch to a mixed bouquet of freesias, stephanotis, grasses, and other garden materials.

CUT ROSES

The best time to cut roses from the garden is late in the afternoon, or at dusk. The next best time is in the early morning while the air is still cool. Roses cut during the heat of the day will quickly wilt for lack of moisture.

Choose flowers that are just opening or that have opened halfway. Because flowers with few petals unfold more quickly than those with many petals, single blooms will last longer if you pick them when they are barely starting to open. A sampling of flowers at various early stages of bloom will give your arrangement a less uniform, and therefore more interesting, appearance. It's better to leave flowers in full bloom on the plant; they're already near the end of their blooming cycle and will not last long as cut flowers.

A rose blossom, just like the rest of the plant, needs a continual supply of moisture or it will start to wilt. It's a good idea to carry a bucket of tepid water when you cut roses so that you can immediately plunge them into water up to the base of the blooms.

Be somewhat sparing in the amount of foliage you cut with the blossoms if the rose is only two or three years old. Leave the plant with plenty of leaves to support its growth. Once the plant is established, you can cut the stems as long as you want them, although you should leave at least two leaves—each consisting of three, five, or seven leaflets—on the main stem.

Use sharp pruning shears and cut at a 45-degree angle just above a five-leaflet leaf. New growth will originate from the base of this leaf.

Keep the flowers in a cool place out of drafts until you are ready to prepare and arrange them. You can further slow the opening of the buds by keeping them in the refrigerator, in a container filled with water.

Preparing and Caring for Roses in Arrangements

Your impulse may be to simply arrange the flowers in water and enjoy them, but if you use the following procedures the roses will look fresher and last days longer. You can also use these methods with roses from a florist.

Remove all foliage and thorns that will be below water level in the vase; otherwise they will rot, producing bacteria that will shorten the life of the flowers.

An easy way to remove foliage is to wrap several layers of paper towel or cloth around the stem and pull downward. Thorns will break off easily if you gently push them from the side with your thumb. Never scrape the stem with a knife; the injuries to the stem will shorten the life of the flowers.

Give each rose a fresh cut at least ½ inch above the end of the stem. Cut at a sharp angle to expose as much cut surface to the water as possible.

After recutting each stem, immerse it in deep water that is too hot for your hand (about 120° F). Leave the roses in this warm bath until the water cools; then place the entire container in a refrigerator or a cool place for a couple of hours to condition the blooms. (Wilted roses can usually be revived by giving them a fresh cut and subjecting them to this hot tub–icebox treatment.)

When you are ready to arrange the roses, fill a vase with fresh water. Some gardeners add a floral preservative to the water; others use only sterile water; still others swear by a dash of a light soft drink, such as 7-Up or

The tub's flat gray finish provides a perfect foil for the satiny pinks, lavenders, and creams of the roses in this informal bedside bouquet. The arrangement includes hybrid tea 'Sweet Surrender' and floribunda 'French Lace'.

Sprite, in the water. Experiment and see what works best for you. If you do use a floral preservative, follow the directions carefully; too much will shock the roses beyond restoration.

To secure the roses in the vase, use 2-inch wire netting balled into the bottom of the vase, a metal holder, pebbles, or florist's foam. If you choose florist's foam, soak it thoroughly in the water before inserting the flowers. Do not move the stem after placing it in the foam, because air pockets will form at the base of the stem, cutting off the water supply.

As you arrange the flowers, give each one a fresh slanted cut before placing it. Keep the finished bouquet in as cool a place as possible, out of drafts and out of direct sunlight. Moving the arrangement to a sheltered spot outside at night will also prolong its freshness. Add enough fresh water daily to keep the stems immersed up to two thirds of their length. Better yet, change the water every day, adding new preservative. The flowers will last even longer if you recut the bottom of the stems every day or so.

Arranging Roses

The arrangement of flowers is a matter of personal taste. Some gardeners prefer a formal design in a high, triangular shape. Others prefer an English-style mixed flower basket, a very simple arrangement with an Oriental touch, or a lone specimen rose in a bud vase.

Currently the trend is toward more natural bouquets, letting the flowers speak for themselves. Sometimes a little restraint produces a more striking composition—each flower can be appreciated individually and as part of the whole. You can improve the appearance of clusters of floribundas by thinning out the more fully opened flowers, which will allow the others to bloom unrestricted.

Choose a container that fits the mood of the room or the occasion and that is in proportion to the size of the flowers. Gleaming silver or other metal reflects the beauty of roses. A wicker basket is a good choice for a casual arrangement; china, ceramic, glass, or crystal creates a more formal look. An arrangement in a see-through vase is more attractive without a mechanical holder or florist's foam. Tiny teacups, creamers, and other small containers are perfect for miniatures.

Arrange a single variety of rose in one container or mix several varieties together. Roses blend successfully with other garden flowers of complementary or contrasting colors. For greenery, rose foliage is always a sure bet, but you might try adding ferns or camellia, ivy, or any other leaves whose shades and textures please you.

Potpourri

"The rose looks fair, but fairer it we deem for that sweet odor which doth in it live." When Shakespeare wrote those words he may have been thinking of potpourri. This traditional way of preserving the memories of the rose garden is as delightful today as it has been for centuries.

The French named the concoction "rotten pot" because they used the moist method of making potpourri, which involves letting the petals slowly rot in a jar. When the jar was opened, the rose fragrance dispelled the stale atmosphere of the stuffy houses.

Today potpourri is most often made by the dry method, but both methods produce a mixture that can sweeten the air with its heady aroma. Whether you use the dry or moist method, it's easy and fun to experiment with different scents and blends to create your own unique fragrance.

MAKING POTPOURRI

Cut the roses in the early morning after the dew is gone. The fresher the flower, the more of the essential oil that will remain after the flower is dried. The most fragrant cultivars (see page 106) will, of course, yield the most fragrant petals, but also consider roses that will contribute color to your mixture. Potpourri need not be composed exclusively of roses; pick other fragrant garden flowers such as lavender, violets, and freesia to mix with the roses, and add fragrant or colorful leaves and herbs.

Gently pull the petals from the flowers. You may wish to include some small leaves or tiny buds for more texture. Select a place away from strong light, where warm air can circulate, and spread the petals, leaves, and buds on a drying rack—preferably a wooden one, because metal can discolor the petals. Alternatively, place the plant materials flat on layers of paper towels. Stir or turn them every day.

The petals for moist potpourri should be dried for only a few days, just until they are limp, not crisp. Petals for dry mixtures should be completely dried, until they are like cereal flakes.

Dry Potpourri

A few damp petals can spoil a whole batch of dry potpourri. Complete drying usually takes from four days to two weeks, depending on the moisture in the petals and in the air. If you are in a hurry, spread the petals on a cookie sheet and place them in a warm oven (110° F). Leave the door open to allow moisture to escape. Stir the mixture gently or shake the sheet from time to time so that the petals will dry evenly. Drying usually takes only one to two hours; however, the petals lose more of their color than when they are dried slowly.

To turn the petals into potpourri, mix them with spices and other fragrant materials if desired, and add a fixative that will preserve the fragrance. Common fixatives include orrisroot, benzoin, and storax. A quarter pound of any one of these is enough for a 1-quart potpourri.

Nutmeg, cloves, cinnamon sticks, lemon peel, and other ingredients found in the kitchen add a tantalizing aroma to both moist and dry potpourri.

Store the potpourri in a tightly covered container for several weeks until the fragrances blend and mellow. Then move it to attractive containers with removable lids. If you use clear glass containers, you'll have the extra pleasure of being able to see the colors of the contents. Sew the potpourri inside sachets, or little bags, to sweeten drawers and closets.

4 cups dried rose petals and small buds
½ cup dried rose leaves
½ cup dried rose geranium leaves
4 ounces dried orrisroot, coarsely crushed
2 tablespoons dried citrus peel, finely chopped
1 tablespoon whole cloves, crushed
1 tablespoon whole allspice
1 teaspoon anise seed, crushed
1 tablespoon cardamom seed, crushed
1 whole nutmeg, crushed
2 bay leaves, finely broken
4 cinnamon sticks, broken into 1-inch pieces
  Several drops *each*, oils of jasmine, rose geranium, and tuberose

1. In a large opaque container with a tight-fitting lid, place rose petals, buds, and leaves, and the geranium leaves.
2. Mix together gently with your hands the orrisroot, citrus peel, and spices. Add to container.

3. Sprinkle oils on top. Close container tightly and shake it vigorously. Shake it twice a week for about six weeks, by which time the mixture will be well aged, then transfer the potpourri to small decorative boxes and jars.

Moist Potpourri

Moist potpourri has a heavier fragrance and lasts longer than a dry mixture. The slightly dried petals are salted down in a crock—like pickles—with noniodized salt mixed with spices, fragrant oils, and a bit of brandy or perfume. These materials are stirred together daily for about a month until the scents are well blended and mellowed. It's a good idea to keep a weight on top of the petals to draw out all the oils.

When the blend is mellow, pour the potpourri into a large container and mix it well once again. Then place it in small porcelain, silver, or opaque glass containers with lids that can be removed whenever you wish to fill the room with the aroma of a summer day.

Whenever moist potpourri seems dry and is losing its fragrance, pour a small amount of good-quality brandy over the top and mix it in to reactivate the fragrant oils.

Lacy, beribboned sachets filled with dry potpourri freshen closets and drawers.

3 bay leaves
¾ cup noniodized table salt
¼ cup allspice, crushed
¼ cup cloves, mashed
¼ cup brown sugar
4 cups partially dried rose petals
2 cups mixed, partially dried, fragrant garden flowers (such as jasmine, orange blossoms, lavender, or violets)
1 cup dried fragrant leaves (such as rose geranium, lemon verbena, chamomile, or rosemary)
1 tablespoon dried orrisroot, coarsely crushed
2 tablespoons brandy

1. Crush the bay leaves into the salt with a mortar and pestle and mix in the allspice, cloves, and sugar.
2. Blend flower petals and leaves together with orrisroot. Place some of the petal mixture in a large crock that can be covered, and sprinkle it with some of the salt mixture. Continue alternating layers of petals and salt.
3. Add the brandy, then cap the container tightly. Stir the mixture daily. After a month, pour the potpourri into a large bowl and mix thoroughly. Then fill small moistureproof containers.

Encyclopedia of Roses

This illustrated listing of nearly two hundred and fifty varieties of roses will help you choose the ones that are exactly suited to your liking and to your needs.

There are hundreds of different roses from which you can choose if you buy from mail-order suppliers. Local nurseries and garden centers usually have a much more limited selection, but they often carry roses that are particularly suited to your climate and region. When you shop locally, you also have the advantage of being able to see what you are buying.

This chapter contains charts describing nearly two hundred and fifty roses. The first column of each chart gives the name of the rose (with any other names it is known by in parentheses), the year of introduction, and any awards bestowed by the American Rose Society (ARS) or the All-America Rose Selections (AARS) judges. Winners of the James Alexander Gamble Rose Fragrance Medal are also noted.

The second column shows the ARS rating. (See page 33 for an explanation of the rating system.) Some roses, especially the newest varieties, are not rated. The third column describes the flower color, and the fourth column gives further details on the flowers. The last column describes the foliage, growth habit, and any advantages, such as exceptional hardiness, or drawbacks, such as susceptibility to disease.

Starting on page 102 are lists of roses by color, roses for specific landscape uses, and those with specific attributes, such as extraordinary fragrance, long-lasting flowers, and disease resistance. These lists are intended as a helpful starting point for you to select roses for your garden.

Floribunda 'Betty Prior' produces clusters of fragrant carmine-pink blossoms all season long.

Rosa moyesii

Rosa banksiae 'Lutea'

Rosa eglanteria

SPECIES ROSES

Rose, awards	ARS rating*	Flower color	Flower description and blooming habits	Foliage, growth habits, and cultural tips
Rosa banksiae (Lady Banks' Rose)	8.8	Yellow or white	1½"–2" double; prolific heavy clusters; 'Lutea' is yellow; 'Alba Plena' is white and scented; spring to early summer.	Evergreen, small, glossy; climbs to 25'; no thorns; resists aphids and diseases; hardy to -5° F.
Rosa eglanteria (*Rosa rubiginosa,* Sweet Briar Rose, Eglantine)	8.6	Light pink with gold stamens	1½"–2" single; slight fragrance; borne singly or in small clusters; late May to early June; bright red hips.	Small leaves smelling strongly of pippin apples, especially when wet; large, vigorous shrub, 8'–14'; hardy.
Rosa foetida bicolor (Austrian Copper Rose)	8.1	Orange and coppery red with yellow reverse	2"–3" single; borne in sprays along arching branches; very attractive color combination; scent like clean linseed oil (offensive to some people).	Dark green; tall, arching, to 8'; very susceptible to blackspot, but flowers more than compensate; hardy.
Rosa foetida persiana (Persian Yellow Rose)	7.8	Chrome yellow	3" double; packed with petals; midsummer; same scent as Austrian Copper Rose (see above).	Rich green; rounded shrub to 6'; parent of modern yellow roses; susceptible to blackspot.
Rosa glauca (*Rosa rubrifolia*)	8.9	Medium pink with white, starlike center and yellow stamens	1½" single; June; bright red hips.	Soft, gray-green with distinct purple sheen; arching, to 6'; hardy.

* American Rose Society Ratings (see page 33): 10.0—Perfect (not yet achieved); 9.0–9.9—Outstanding; 8.0–8.9—Excellent; 7.0–7.9—Good; 6.0–6.9—Fair; 5.9 and lower—Of questionable value. N.R. indicates that a rating has not yet been established.

Rosa rugosa

Rosa foetida bicolor

Rosa wichuraiana

SPECIES ROSES

Rose, awards	ARS rating*	Flower color	Flower description and blooming habits	Foliage, growth habits, and cultural tips
Rosa hugonis (Father Hugo Rose)	8.1	Medium yellow	2½" semidouble; sweet fragrance; borne singly during May and June.	Small, gray-green leaves; large, 8' × 8'; drooping branches; very hardy.
Rosa laevigata (Cherokee Rose)	7.4	White with gold stamens	3"–4" single; scent of gardenias; borne in clusters in spring.	Glossy; trails or climbs 15'–50'; naturalized in South.
Rosa moyesii	N.R.	Red with creamy stamens	2"–3" single; slight scent; blooms once, in mid-June.	Delicate, lacy; large, awkward, to 12' × 10'; hardy once established.
Rosa rugosa (Japanese Rose, Ramanas Rose, Rugosa Rose)	8.4	Carmine-mauve with yellow stamens	2½"–4" semidouble; cinnamon fragrance; borne singly or in small clusters; repeats even while setting hips; large round red-orange hips.	Rich green, deeply textured; upright, 3'–6'; hardy; disease resistant; suckers; good for hedges.
Rosa spinosissima (Scotch Rose, Burnet Rose)	7.7	Cream	1¼"–2" single; fragrant; numerous along stems; garden forms available with white, yellow, pink, or purple flowers; black hips.	Suckering habit; low growing; hardy; good as ground cover.
Rosa virginiana	8.0	Medium pink with gold stamens	2" single; sweet fragrance; borne singly or in small clusters; a mass of blooms in late June.	Glossy; dense shrub, to 6'; colorful in fall; fairly hardy.
Rosa wichuraiana (Memorial Rose)	7.0	White	1½"–2" single; slightly fragrant; borne in clusters during July.	Glossy, bright green; prostrate with creeping branches to 15'.

Blanc Double de Coubert

Carefree Wonder

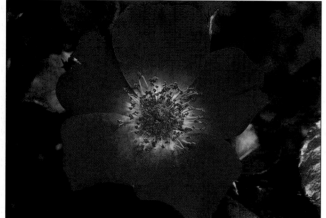

Dortmund

Fair Bianca

MODERN SHRUB ROSES

Rose, year of introduction, awards	ARS rating*	Flower color	Flower description and blooming habits	Foliage, growth habits, and cultural tips
All That Jazz (1991), AARS 1992	8.2	Coral-salmon blend	Semidouble, cupped; in loose, large sprays of 3–5 blooms.	Medium or dark green, glossy; upright, bushy, medium height.
Blanc Double de Coubert (1892), Hybrid rugosa	8.3	White	2"–3" semidouble; very fragrant; papery, cupped petals.	Glossy, corrugated; 4' × 5'; disease resistant; hardy.
Buff Beauty (1939), Hybrid musk	8.3	Apricot yellow	3" double; strong tea scent; profuse; recurrent.	Dark green, glossy; vigorous, arching, to 6'; good for banks, fences.
Carefree Wonder (1990), AARS 1991	N.R.	Medium pink with lighter pink reverse	Medium, double, flat; in sprays of 1–4.	Medium, bright green, semiglossy; disease resistant, winter hardy.
Constance Spry (1961)	7.8	Light pink	3½"–5" double; strong scent; midsummer.	Dark green; large, vigorous, 7' × 7', arching; good as screen or on fence.
Dortmund (1955), Kordesii	9.1	Strawberry red with white center	2½"–3½" single; slight fragrance; large clusters throughout season.	Dark green, glossy, hollylike; vigorous, trailing canes to 10'; very disease resistant; hardy; tolerates some shade; can be grown as a large shrub, pegged as a ground cover, or used as a climber.
Fair Bianca (1983)	8.2	Light yellow to white	Medium size, very double, flat; fragrant.	Light green, semiglossy; upright.
Frau Dagmar Hartopp (Fru Dagmar Hastrup), (1914), Hybrid rugosa	8.5	Silvery pink with golden stamens	3" single; strong fragrance; continuous clusters; large crimson hips.	Dark green, textured; compact, 2½'–3'; hardy; good low hedge.
Golden Wings (1956), ARS Gold Medal Certificate 1958	7.9	Sulfur yellow	4½" semidouble; lightly scented; repeats.	Deep yellowish green; free branching, compact, 4' × 4'; hardy.

All That Jazz

Meidomonac

Kathleen

Golden Wings

MODERN SHRUB ROSES

Rose, year of introduction, awards	ARS rating*	Flower color	Flower description and blooming habits	Foliage, growth habits, and cultural tips
Kathleen (1922), Hybrid musk	8.1	Blush pink with gold stamens	1"–1½" single; rich apple-blossom scent; very free blooming; orange hips.	Glossy; 6'–15', semiclimber with training; can also be used as a shrub; very disease resistant; quite hardy.
Meidomonac (Bonica '82), (1981), AARS 1987	9.1	Medium pink center, light pink edges	3" double; often borne in clusters of 20 or more; profuse; repeats; light fragrance.	Small, dark green, semiglossy; vigorous, bushy, to 5' × 5'; best in cooler summer climates; disease resistant; hardy; excellent for hedges and mass plantings; only shrub given AARS award.
Nevada (1927), Hybrid moyesii	8.2	White (sometimes tinted pink)	4"–5" semidouble; no scent; hundreds of blooms almost hiding foliage; recurrent.	Soft green, small leaves; vigorous, arching, rounded, to 7'; hardy.
Otello (Auslo),(1990)	7.9	Clear red	Very large; strongly fragrant; cupped petals; continuous clusters.	Dark green; vigorous, bushy growth.
Pink Grootendorst (1923), Hybrid rugosa	7.6	Clear pink	Small double; carnationlike; no scent; good cut; recurrent.	Small, wrinkled leaves; bushy, thorny, to 4'; hardy.
Sparrieshoop (1953)	8.6	Light pink	4" single to semidouble; very fragrant; abundant, in clusters or singly; repeats.	Leathery; red thorns; upright, vigorous; can be used as a climber.
Sunny June (1952)	7.7	Deep canary yellow	3"–3½" single; large clusters; slight spicy fragrance.	Dark green, glossy; tall, upright, to 8'; can be used as a shrub or pillar rose.
White Meideland (Alba Meideland, Blanc Meillandecor), (1986)	8.3	White	Very full (over 40 petals); no fragrance; large.	Dark green, medium-sized, glossy leaves; spreading.
Wise Portia (1983)	8.5	Mauve	Large double; very fragrant.	Dark green, semiglossy; bushy.

Complicata

Rosa Mundi

Autumn Damask

Superb Tuscan

OLD GARDEN ROSES

Rose, year of introduction, awards	ARS rating*	Flower color	Flower description and blooming habits	Foliage, growth habits, and cultural tips
GALLICA				
Apothecary's Rose (*Rosa gallica officinalis,* Double French Rose, Red Rose of Lancaster), (before 1600)	8.6	Deep pink with yellow stamens	2"–3" semidouble; strong fragrance; used in potpourri and attar of roses; midsummer.	Rough, dark green; branching habit, to 4'; suckers; hardy.
Complicata (date unknown)	8.4	Pink with white eye and yellow stamens	5" single; blooms along length of branch; spectacular in full flower.	Large, light green leaves; vigorous shrub or pillar, to 6'; can be rampant.
Rosa Mundi (*Rosa gallica versicolor*), (possibly before 1581)	8.6	Striped red, pink, and white	2"–3" semidouble; light fragrance; flaring petals.	Rough, dark green; low, to 3', sprawling; sport of *Rosa gallica;* hardy.
Superb Tuscan (before 1848)	8.2	Dark crimson-purple	4"–5" semidouble; slight fragrance; velvety.	Rough, dark green; vigorous bush, 2'–3'; hardy.
DAMASK				
Autumn Damask (*Rosa damascena semperflorens*), (before 1819)	8.0	Pink	3½" double; very fragrant; useful for potpourri and rose oil; crumpled petals; recurrent in warm climates.	Rough, light green; vigorous, to 5'; hardy.

Fantin-Latour

Celestial

Königin von Dänemark

OLD GARDEN ROSES

Rose, year of introduction, awards	ARS rating*	Flower color	Flower description and blooming habits	Foliage, growth habits, and cultural tips
Madame Hardy (1832)	9.2	White	2½"–3½" double; strong fragrance; petals cupped around green center; borne in clusters; spring.	Clear green; thickly foliaged, 4'–6'; hardy.
York and Lancaster (*Rosa damascena versicolor*), (before 1629)	7.3	White and pale pink	1½"–2½" semidouble; moderate fragrance; sometimes pink, sometimes white, sometimes having different-colored petals but not striped.	Light gray-green; vigorous, to 5'; hardy.
ALBA				
Celestial (Céleste), (late 1700s)	8.6	Soft pink	3½" semidouble; sweet fragrance; half-opened buds; borne in clusters; blooms once a year; of particular beauty.	Blue-green; vigorous, to 6'; known for its unique complement of foliage and flowers.
Great Maiden's Blush (*Rosa alba incarnata*), (before 1738)	8.5	White tinged pink	2"–3" double; moderate fragrance; early summer.	Gray-green; vigorous, to 5'; hardy.
Königin von Dänemark (Queen of Denmark), (1826)	8.3	Flesh pink with darker center	2½"–4" double; strong fragrance; dark pink buds; blooms once a year.	Blue-green; loose, spreading, to 7'; hardy.
CENTIFOLIA				
Fantin-Latour (date unknown)	8.2	Soft pink	2"–3" double; delicate fragrance; flat; prolific; summer.	Dark green, smooth; arching, to 5'; benefits from support; hardy.

Crested Moss

Rose de Meaux

Duchesse de Brabant

OLD GARDEN ROSES

Rose, year of introduction, awards	ARS rating*	Flower color	Flower description and blooming habits	Foliage, growth habits, and cultural tips
Rose de Meaux (*Rosa centifolia pomponia*, Pompon Rose), (1789)	7.0	Medium pink	1"–1½" double; resembling pom-poms; strong fragrance.	Light green; arching, to 3'; dense; twiggy growth requires pruning; hardy.
MOSS				
Communis (Common Moss, Old Pink Moss, Pink Moss), (late 1600s)	7.7	Rose pink	2"–3" double; strong fragrance; reddish, mossed buds have pine scent.	Dull green; rounded, arching, to 6'; hardy.
Crested Moss (*Rosa centifolia cristata*, Chapeau de Napoléon), (1827)	7.9	Medium pink	2"–3" double; moderate fragrance; heavy frill of moss on sepals; opening buds are especially beautiful.	Medium green, delicate; rounded, arching, to 7'; hardy.
Salet (1854)	8.1	Rosy pink	2"–3½" double; strong musk fragrance; opens flat; some recurrence.	Light green; sturdy, 6'–10'; hardy.
CHINA				
Hermosa (1840)	7.7	Light blush pink	1"–3" double; moderate fragrance; recurrent.	Gray-green; to 3'; tender.
Old Blush (Parson's Pink China, Old Pink Daily, Old Pink Monthly, Common Monthly), (1752)	8.3	Two-tone pink	1½"–2½" semidouble; moderate fragrance; borne in clusters; recurrent.	Soft green; to 5'; tender.
BOURBON				
Honorine de Brabant (1800s)	7.6	Pale lilac-pink spotted and streaked with mauve and crimson	3½"–4" double; raspberry fragrance; streaked and spotted petals; often a second bloom.	Light green, smooth; rampant, to 5'.
La Reine Victoria (1872)	7.8	Rich pink	1½"–2½" double; delicate fragrance; repeats.	Narrow, smooth; erect, to 6'; appreciates support; tender.

Frau Karl Druschki

Comte de Chambord

Communis

Souvenir de la Malmaison

Sombreuil

OLD GARDEN ROSES

Rose, year of introduction, awards	ARS rating*	Flower color	Flower description and blooming habits	Foliage, growth habits, and cultural tips
Souvenir de la Malmaison (Queen of Beauty and Fragrance), (1843)	8.4	Creamy flesh with rosy center	1½"–4" double; spicy fragrance; fades to almost white; recurrent.	Medium green; shrub or pillar, vigorous, to 6'; tender.
PORTLAND				
Comte de Chambord (1860)	8.0	Pink-tinted lilac	3"–4½" double; fragrant; recurrent.	Deep green; vigorous, erect, to 4'; hardy.
TEA				
Duchesse de Brabant (Comtesse de Labarthe, Comtesse Ouwaroff), (1857)	8.2	Soft to bright rosy pink	2"–3" double; rich fragrance; upright, tuliplike buds; free blooming.	Glossy; upright, to 4'; quite tender.
Maman Cochet (1893)	7.2	Pale pink with lemon yellow base	3"–4" double; moderate fragrance; single flowering in June.	Dark green, glossy; to 4'; quite tender.
Sombreuil (1850)	8.8	Ivory white	4" very double; strong tea fragrance; hundreds of furled petals; pendulous blooms.	Light green, glossy; moderately vigorous climber, to 8'–10'; good on arbors; best viewed from below; tender.
NOISETTE				
Lamarque (1830)	8.6	White with yellow center	2" double; light fragrance; recurrent.	Light green; vigorous climber, to 15'; tender.
HYBRID PERPETUAL				
Baronne Prévost (1842)	8.5	Rosy pink, shading lighter	3"–4" double; moderate fragrance; borne in clusters; repeats.	Medium green; vigorous, to 5'; fairly hardy.
Ferdinand Pichard (1921)	7.4	Striped pink and scarlet	2½"–4" double; little scent; spring and fall.	Yellowish green; to 5'; responds to pegging if low spreader is desired.
Frau Karl Druschki (1901)	7.8	Snow white, center sometimes blush pink	Large double; no scent but attractive blooms and habit.	Dark green; vigorous; hardy; susceptible to disease; can be used as a climber in mild climates.

Marchesa Boccella

Stanwell Perpetual

Reine des Violettes

OLD GARDEN ROSES

Rose, year of introduction, awards	ARS rating*	Flower color	Flower description and blooming habits	Foliage, growth habits, and cultural tips
Général Jacqueminot (General Jack, Jack Rose), (1853)	7.1	Dark red, whitish reverse	2½"–4" double; velvety petals; very fragrant; strong stems; spring and fall.	Rich green; vigorous, to 6'.
Marchesa Boccella (1842)	8.9	Delicate pink with blush edges	Large; full; more petals than other hybrid perpetuals; stiff, erect stems.	Dwarf, robust habit.
Reine des Violettes (1860)	8.0	Violet red	Large double; very fragrant; heavy repeat bloomer.	Silvery green; nearly thornless; 6'–8' ✕ 4'; can be used as a climber.
HYBRIDS OF SPECIES				
Félicité et Perpétué (1828), Hybrid sempervirens	6.9	White blush to pale cream	1"–1½" double; delicate primrose fragrance; large clusters; blooms once a year.	Semievergreen, glossy, blue-green; vigorous, 12'–15'; disease resistant; fairly hardy; can be grown as a screen or pegged as a ground cover.
Frühlingsgold (Spring Gold), (1937), Hybrid spinosissima	7.6	Creamy yellow	3½"–5" single; strong fragrance; a magnificent display in spring, sometimes a second in fall.	Gray-green; strong, dense, to 7' ✕ 7'; hardy.
Harison's Yellow (around 1830), Hybrid foetida	8.0	Bright yellow	2"–3" semidouble; yeasty aroma; free flowering during May and June.	Gray-green, delicate; 8'–10' tall and spreading; thorny; very hardy.
Mermaid (1918), Hybrid bracteata	8.3	Pale sulfur yellow	5"–6" single; slight fragrance; free blooming.	Glossy, dark green; vigorous, to over 20'; thorny; tender; resistant to blackspot.
Stanwell Perpetual (1938), Hybrid spinosissima	8.6	Blush fading to white	3½" double; strong fragrance; creased petals; summer-long blooming.	Grayish green, thorny; arching, to 6'; often rather loose, straggling growth if not supported.

Captain Harry Stebbings

Chicago Peace

Brandy

Brigadoon

HYBRID TEA ROSES

Rose, year of introduction, awards	ARS rating*	Flower color	Flower description and blooming habits	Foliage, growth habits, and cultural tips
Bewitched (1967), AARS 1967	7.2	Pure pink	5" double; spicy fragrance; good cut.	Glossy; tall, bushy; disease resistant; easy to grow.
Brandy (1981), AARS 1982	7.3	Golden apricot	Large double; tea fragrance.	Semiglossy; strong, bushy; disease resistant.
Bride's Dream (1985)	8.0	Light pink	Large, double, high centered; borne singly; fragrant.	Deep green; large, tall, upright.
Brigadoon (1991), AARS 1992	N.R.	Pink and cream	4½"–5" very double; spicy fragrance.	Dark green semiglossy; slightly spreading, medium to tall.
Captain Harry Stebbings (1980)	8.1	Deep cerise-pink	5"–6" double; very well formed; very fruity fragrance; good cut.	Very large, dark green, leathery leaves; upright, medium to tall; very hardy and vigorous; susceptible to powdery mildew.
Cary Grant (1987)	7.3	Vibrant orange with lighter shading	4"–6" double; can produce many blooms or be stingy, depending on weather; spicy fragrance; long lasting; good cut.	Medium green, semiglossy, very thorny; medium height, slightly spreading; somewhat susceptible to powdery mildew.
Century Two (1971)	8.0	Medium pink	5"–6" double; moderate fragrance; abundant; repeats quickly; good cut.	Dark green, leathery; upright, medium to tall; susceptible to disease.
Charlotte Armstrong (1940), AARS 1941	8.0	Deep pink, becoming red	3"–4" double; light tea fragrance; free blooming on long stems; good cut.	Dark green, leathery; very vigorous, medium height.
Chicago Peace (1962)	7.7	Pink with canary-yellow base	5"–5½" double; slight fragrance; more intense color than 'Peace'; good cut.	Glossy, leathery; vigorous, upright, bushy, medium height.

Chrysler Imperial

Electron

First Prize

Dolly Parton

Dublin

HYBRID TEA ROSES

Rose, year of introduction, awards	ARS rating*	Flower color	Flower description and blooming habits	Foliage, growth habits, and cultural tips
Chrysler Imperial (1952), AARS 1953, ARS Gold Medal Certificate 1956, James Alexander Gamble Rose Fragrance Medal 1965	7.8	Crimson with darker shading	4½"–5" double; heavy, spicy fragrance; moderate blooming; long stems; good cut.	Dark green; upright, to 4'; needs summer heat to perform well.
Color Magic (1978), AARS 1978	8.2	Ivory to deep rose	6"–7" double; color darkens with age; slight fragrance.	Dark green, glossy; vigorous, medium height; disease resistant; needs extra winter protection in cold climates.
Confidence (1951)	7.5	Light pink to yellow blend	3"–5" double; intense fragrance; profuse.	Dark green, leathery; vigorous growth, to 4'; very disease resistant.
Crimson Glory (1935), James Alexander Gamble Rose Fragrance Medal 1961	6.8	Deep crimson with purple shadings	3"–4" double; heavy old-fashioned fragrance; blooms best in warm climates.	Dark green, glossy; vigorous and spreading, to 4'.
Dainty Bess (1925)	9.0	Rosy pink with maroon stamens	3"–4" single; moderate fragrance; ruffled edges.	Abundant, leathery; vigorous, upright, to 4'; hardy.
Dolly Parton (1984), ARS Trial Grounds winner	7.4	Luminous orange-red	6" double; very fragrant; good cut.	Medium green, semiglossy; upright.
Double Delight (1977), AARS 1977, James Alexander Gamble Rose Fragrance Medal 1986	8.9	Creamy white, becoming red	5½"–6" double; heavy, spicy fragrance; prolific; excellent cut; amount of red depends on heat, increases with age.	Dark green, glossy; spreading, quite bushy, medium height; somewhat tender; disease resistant.

Fragrant Cloud

Garden Party

Folklore

HYBRID TEA ROSES

Rose, year of introduction, awards	ARS rating*	Flower color	Flower description and blooming habits	Foliage, growth habits, and cultural tips
Dublin (1982)	8.5	Deep raspberry red with darker edges	5"–6" double exhibition blooms; very strong fragrance.	Matte green; slightly spreading, medium to tall.
Duet (1960), AARS 1961	7.6	Light and dark pink	2"–4" double; petals light pink inside, darker outside; slight scent; prolific clusters; good color retention.	Glossy, hollylike; vigorous, bushy, 4' or taller; disease resistant; excellent for hedges; easy to grow.
Electron (1970), AARS 1973	7.7	Rosy pink	3"–5" double; fragrant; very free blooming; good retention of intense color.	Lush, dark green; vigorous and bushy, to 3'; disease resistant.
Elina (Peaudouce), (1984)	8.6	Pale yellow to creamy white	5"–6" very double; borne singly and in small clusters; very floriferous.	Dark green, glossy, large; very vigorous, medium to tall, bushy; disease resistant, hardy.
Elizabeth Taylor (1986)	8.8	Hot pink	4"–5½" double; usually borne singly; fragrant; repeats well.	Dark green, semiglossy; upright, vigorous; susceptible to powdery mildew and blackspot.
First Prize (1970), AARS 1970	9.1	Rosy pink with ivory center	6" double; moderate fragrance; abundant; long stems; excellent cut.	Dark green, leathery; medium height, spreading; resistant to blackspot; tender; easy to grow.
Folklore (1977)	8.5	Orange, yellow reverse	4"–5" double, well formed; very fragrant; long lasting; good cut.	Medium green; very tall and upright; disease resistant; very hardy; makes a good screen; easy to grow.
Fragrant Cloud (Duftwolke), (1963), James Alexander Gamble Rose Fragrance Medal 1969	8.3	Coral red, becoming geranium red	5" double; color darkens with age; heavy tea fragrance; free blooming.	Dark green, glossy; vigorous, upright, medium height; easy to grow.

Granada

Helmut Schmidt

Maid of Honour

Keepsake

Honor

HYBRID TEA ROSES

Rose, year of introduction, awards	ARS rating*	Flower color	Flower description and blooming habits	Foliage, growth habits, and cultural tips
Garden Party (1959), AARS 1960	8.2	Pale yellow fading to white and light pink at edges	4"–5" double; slight fragrance; free blooming; good cut.	Dark green, semiglossy; vigorous, bushy, medium height; resistant to diseases except sometimes powdery mildew; very hardy; easy to grow.
Granada (1963), AARS 1964, James Alexander Gamble Rose Fragrance Medal 1968	8.3	Rose, red, and yellow blend	4"–5" double; rich fragrance; long lasting; free blooming.	Hollylike; vigorous, upright, medium height; resistant to blackspot.
Great Scott (1991)	7.8	Clear medium pink	5"–6", repeats well, slight fragrance.	Large, matte green; medium to tall; disease resistant, hardy, easy to grow.
Helmut Schmidt (1979)	N.R.	Medium yellow	3"–4" double; borne 1–3 per cluster; fragrant.	Upright, bushy.
Honor (1980), AARS 1980	7.5	Pure white	5" double; light fragrance; prolific, large clusters.	Olive green; vigorous, upright, tall; good disease resistance.
Keepsake (Esmeralda), (1983)	8.4	Silvery pink, blended from deep to light pink	5"–6" very double; well formed; very fragrant; repeats frequently.	Deep green, glossy; medium height; very disease resistant; can be somewhat tender; best in cool-summer climates.
Korlingo (Kordes' Rose Kardinal), (1986)	8.5	Scarlet red	3"–3½" double, very long lasting, well formed; fragrant.	Semiglossy dark green; medium height, upright.

Mister Lincoln

Mikado

Miss All-American Beauty

Loving Memory

HYBRID TEA ROSES

Rose, year of introduction, awards	ARS rating*	Flower color	Flower description and blooming habits	Foliage, growth habits, and cultural tips
Lady X (1966)	8.3	Mauve	Large double; slight fragrance; abundant; good cut.	Dark green; tall, strong, upright; very hardy.
Loving Memory (Burgund '81), (1981)	7.1	Medium red	Very large, very double; loosely formed; slight fragrance.	Medium green, semiglossy; upright, bushy, medium to tall; hardy; disease resistant.
Maid of Honour (1986)	7.6	Pale buff yellow	4", many petals; borne singly and in clusters.	Large, dark green, semiglossy; upright, medium height.
Marijke Koopman (1979)	8.9	Medium pink	3"–4" double; borne in clusters; fragrant.	Dark green, leathery; upright, bushy, medium height; very hardy and disease resistant.
Midas Touch (1993), AARS 1994	N.R.	Deep yellow	4"; light musk fragrance.	Large, dark green, semiglossy; upright, bushy; medium height.
Mikado (1988), AARS 1988	7.1	Brilliant red, washed with yellow reverse	4"–5" double; light, spicy fragrance; slow to repeat.	Glossy green; vigorous, upright, freely branching; very good resistance to powdery mildew, above average to blackspot; prone to rust.
Miss All-American Beauty (Maria Callas), (1965), AARS 1968	8.2	Dark pink	4"–5" double; heavy tea fragrance; free blooming; good color retention.	Leathery; bushy, upright, to 4'; disease resistant.
Mister Lincoln (1964), AARS 1965	8.8	Dark red	4½"–6" double; rich, deep fragrance; abundant; long stemmed; good cut.	Dark green, leathery; sturdy, upright, to over 4'; hardy; disease resistant; easy to grow.

Rio Samba

Olympiad

Precious Platinum

HYBRID TEA ROSES

Rose, year of introduction, awards	ARS rating*	Flower color	Flower description and blooming habits	Foliage, growth habits, and cultural tips
Miyabi (1977)	7.6	Creamy white	4"–4½" double; slightly fragrant.	Medium green, matte; bushy; slightly spreading; medium height; disease resistant.
Mon Cheri (1981), AARS 1982	7.1	Pink aging to dark red	5" double; profuse; light, spicy fragrance.	Semiglossy; vigorous; bushy, medium height.
Olympiad (1983), AARS 1984	9.1	Crimson	4"–5" double; little fragrance; borne singly or in small clusters on long, strong stems; abundant.	Medium green; bushy, 3'–5'; good disease resistance; fairly hardy.
Oregold (1975), AARS 1975	6.7	Deep yellow	5" double; slight fragrance; colorfast; continuous.	Dark, glossy; vigorous, upright, to 4'; disease resistant.
Osiria (1978)	6.5	Dark red, white reverse	4½"–6" double; intensely fragrant; repeats well.	Dark green, glossy; upright, medium to tall; good disease resistance.
Papa Meilland (1963), James Alexander Gamble Rose Fragrance Medal 1974	7.3	Crimson	Large double; velvety petals; heavy, old-fashioned fragrance; prolific.	Olive green, glossy, leathery; vigorous, upright; susceptible to powdery mildew.
Paradise (1978), AARS 1979	8.3	Silvery lavender with ruby edging	5" semidouble; light fragrance; red spreads into lavender as flower unfolds; good cut.	Glossy, deep green; vigorous, very bushy, to 3½'; disease resistant.

Osiria

Perfect Moment

Pristine

HYBRID TEA ROSES

Rose, year of introduction, awards	ARS rating*	Flower color	Flower description and blooming habits	Foliage, growth habits, and cultural tips
Pascali (1963), AARS 1969	8.1	Cream	3"–4" double; slight fragrance; abundant; good cut.	Dark, glossy; vigorous, bushy, to 4'; very disease resistant.
Peace (1945), AARS 1946, ARS Gold Medal Certificate 1948 (the first winner of this award)	8.6	Yellow with pink edges	5"–6" double; slight fragrance; voted the world's favorite rose; good cut.	Very dark green, glossy; very vigorous, bushy, tall, to 4'; disease resistant; hardy.
Perfect Moment (1990), AARS 1991	7.5	Red and yellow	3"–3½" double, cupped; slight fragrance.	Medium, bright green, semiglossy; upright, bushy, medium height.
Perfume Delight (1973), AARS 1974	7.6	Deep pink	4½"–5" double; heavy, spicy fragrance; abundant.	Large, leathery, olive green; bushy, upright, 3'–4'; disease resistant.
Precious Platinum (Opa Pötschke, Red Star), (1974)	7.5	Blood red	5"–6" double; very prolific; slightly fragrant; good cut.	Glossy, leathery; medium to tall, upright; exceptionally hardy and disease resistant.
Pristine (1978)	9.2	Ivory with pink wash	5"–6" double; slight fragrance; prolific.	Glossy, dark reddish green; medium height, spreading; very disease resistant; very hardy; easy to grow.
Rio Samba (Jackrite), (1993), AARS 1993	N.R.	Yellow with red edges	Large semidouble; slight fragrance.	Medium, dark green, matte; upright and bushy, medium height.

Silverado

Sheer Elegance

Tiffany

HYBRID TEA ROSES

Rose, year of introduction, awards	ARS rating*	Flower color	Flower description and blooming habits	Foliage, growth habits, and cultural tips
Royal Highness (1962), AARS 1963	8.2	Light pink	5"–5½" double; heavy tea fragrance; good form; abundant; good cut.	Deep green, leathery; bushy, medium height, 2½'–4'; somewhat tender; resistant to powdery mildew.
Secret (1994), AARS 1994	N.R.	White overlaid with pink	4" double, borne singly; extremely fragrant.	Large, medium green, semiglossy; bushy growth, tall.
Sheer Bliss (1987), AARS 1987	7.8	White flushed pink	4"–6" double; moderate spicy fragrance.	Medium green; upright, medium height; somewhat tender; disease resistant.
Sheer Elegance (1990), AARS 1991		Orange-pink blend, deeper color on edges	4"–4½" very double, classic form.	Large, dark green, glossy; upright, medium height; disease resistant, hardy.
Silverado (1987)	7.5	Soft silver blushed ruby, white reverse	3½"–4½" double; usually borne singly; slightly fragrant; good cut.	Dark green; medium height, bushy; vigorous.
Suffolk (1983)	8.5	White with raspberry edges	4"–4½" very double, well formed.	Large, medium green; upright, very bushy growth; medium to tall; disease resistant, hardy.
Sutter's Gold (1950), AARS 1950, James Alexander Gamble Rose Fragrance Medal 1966	5.7	Golden orange tinged with salmon pink	4"–5" double; heavy, fruity fragrance.	Dark green, glossy, leathery; very vigorous, spreading, 3'–4'; color retention best in cool weather; very disease resistant.
Swarthmore (1963)	8.1	Rosy red	4" double; slight fragrance; many continuous blossoms; long lasting; good cut.	Dark green, leathery; very vigorous, to over 4'; very hardy.
Tiffany (1954), AARS 1955, James Alexander Gamble Rose Fragrance Medal 1962	8.3	Rose to pink	4"–5" double; exceptional fragrance; beautiful buds; free blooming; long lasting; good cut.	Dark green; very vigorous, upright, to over 4'; best performance in warm climates; disease resistant.

Sutter's Gold

Tropicana

Touch of Class

HYBRID TEA ROSES

Rose, year of introduction, awards	ARS rating*	Flower color	Flower description and blooming habits	Foliage, growth habits, and cultural tips
Touch of Class (1984), AARS 1986	9.5	Medium pink, shaded coral and cream, lightens with age	4"–6" double; slight fragrance; very well formed, prolific, long lasting; good cut.	Dark green, semiglossy; upright, medium height; slightly tender; susceptible to powdery mildew.
Trojan Victory (Korperki), (1986)	7.5	Dark red	3½"–4" very double, high centers, classical form; very floriferous.	Medium, bright green, semiglossy; very tall, very bushy; disease resistant, hardy.
Tropicana (Super Star), (1960), AARS 1963, ARS Gold Medal Certificate 1967	7.9	Coral-orange	4"–5" double; strong, fruity fragrance; colorfast; abundant; good cut.	Dark green, glossy, leathery; vigorous, 4'–5', spreading; easy to grow, although somewhat prone to powdery mildew.
Uncle Joe (1971)	7.7	Dark red	4"–6" very double; opens slowly over days; good cut.	Dark green, leathery; upright, tall, very vigorous; very hardy and disease resistant.
Voodoo (1986), AARS 1986	7.0	Blend of salmon, yellow, orange and red fading to pink	5"–6" double; sweet fragrance; abundant.	Dark green, very glossy, leathery; upright, vigorous, tall; hardy; disease resistant.
White Masterpiece (1969)	7.5	White	6" double; light, sweet fragrance; extremely well formed; continuous blooms; good cut.	Deep green, glossy; medium height, to 3', spreading; disease resistant.
White Success (1985)	7.8	Pure white	3"–4" double; well formed; borne profusely on short stems; no scent.	Dark green, semiglossy; relatively short and upright, occasionally spreading; needs winter protection; very disease resistant.

French Lace

Eyepaint

Apricot Nectar

FLORIBUNDA AND POLYANTHA ROSES   Cultivars marked with a dagger (†) are polyanthas.

Rose, year of introduction, awards	ARS rating*	Flower color	Flower description and blooming habits	Foliage, growth habits, and cultural tips
Anabell (1972)	8.5	Bright tangerine and silver blend	4" double; borne in huge clusters of 15 or more; fragrant; good cut.	Medium green, glossy; short to medium height, bushy, upright; hardy; disease resistant.
Angel Face (1968), AARS 1969	8.3	Mauve-lavender	4" double; heavy, old-fashioned fragrance; good cut.	Dark green, leathery; compact, bushy, to 2'; disease resistant.
Apricot Nectar (1965), AARS 1966	8.1	Apricot-pink with golden base	4"–4½" double; clusters of 3 or more; very fruity apricot fragrance.	Dark green, glossy, leathery; very vigorous, bushy; tender; susceptible to blackspot.
Betty Prior (1935)	8.2	Carmine-pink	2"–3" single; moderate fragrance; very profuse and continuous.	Glossy, dark; very vigorous, 4'–5'; hardy; disease resistant.
†Cécile Brünner (Sweetheart Rose, Mignon), (1881)	8.0	Bright pink on yellow	1"–1½" double; moderately sweet fragrance; exquisite buds; continuous.	Tiny, dark green, glossy leaves; few thorns; upright, to 3'.
Cherish (1980), AARS 1980	8.0	Coral pink	3"–4" double, almost hybrid tea size; light cinnamon fragrance; continual and abundant over a long season; good cut.	Glossy, deep green; vigorous, spreading, medium height.
†China Doll (1946)	8.2	Rosy pink with yellow base	1"–2" double; slight fragrance; continual masses of blooms cover plant.	Leathery; low growing, under 18"; good for borders, containers.
Class Act (1988), AARS 1989	N.R.	Pure white	4" double; borne in clusters; slight fragrance.	Dark green, glossy; medium to tall, upright, very vigorous.
Dicky (1983), Gold Medal, Royal National Rose Society	8.8	Reddish salmon-pink, lighter on reverse	Double, in large clusters.	Medium green, glossy; bushy, short to medium height; disease resistant, hardy.
Esperanza (1966)	7.1	Bright red	Large semidouble, flat; borne in big clusters.	Dark bronzy green, leathery, glossy; medium to tall, bushy, vigorous, upright; hardy; disease resistant.

First Edition

Cherish

Angel Face

FLORIBUNDA AND POLYANTHA ROSES

Cultivars marked with a dagger (†) are polyanthas.

Rose, year of introduction, awards	ARS rating*	Flower color	Flower description and blooming habits	Foliage, growth habits, and cultural tips
Europeana (1963), AARS 1968	9.0	Dark crimson	3" double; slight scent; many heavy clusters.	Reddish green; short, bushy; disease resistant; easy to grow in all climates; good hedge, foliage and flowers down to the ground.
Eyepaint (Tapis Persan), (1975)	8.1	Red blend with golden stamens	2½" single; slight scent; continuous.	Dense, dark green; tall, spreading; susceptible to blackspot; good hedge.
First Edition (1976), AARS 1977	8.6	Coral, shaded orange	2½" semidouble; slight fragrance; continual bloom; color deepens in cool climates; good cut.	Glossy, leathery, olive green; vigorous, medium height; good for containers.
French Lace (1981), AARS 1982	8.2	Ivory white with peach and pink tones	3"–4" double; slight fragrance; clusters of 1–8 on single stems; continual bloom.	Dark green, hollylike; medium height, bushy; good disease resistance.
Gene Boerner (1968), AARS 1969	8.5	Deep pink	2½"–3½" double; slight tea fragrance; free blooming.	Light green, glossy; medium to tall, upright; good disease resistance.
H. C. Andersen (Hans Christian Andersen, Touraine), (1986)		Dark red	Semidouble, cupped, in large sprays.	Medium, dark green, glossy; bushy, medium to tall; vigorous, hardy.
Iceberg (Schneewittchen), (1958)	8.7	Pure white	2"–4" double; pleasant scent; large clusters of long-lasting blooms.	Glossy, light green; medium to tall, round, vigorous; extremely hardy; disease resistant; attractive hedge.
Impatient (1984), AARS 1984	7.8	Orange-red	3" double; slight fragrance; clusters on long stems; excellent repeat bloomer.	New growth mahogany-colored, turning dark green; 3'–4', mounding.
Intrigue (1984), AARS 1984	7.3	Deep plum	3" double; rich, old-fashioned fragrance; small clusters; free blooming.	Glossy, dark green; medium height, upright; resistant to powdery mildew.
Ivory Fashion (1958), AARS 1959	8.6	Ivory	4"–4½" semidouble; moderate fragrance; free flowering.	Leathery; vigorous, upright, to 2'–3'; disease resistant.

Margo Koster

Sunsprite

Sexy Rexy

FLORIBUNDA AND POLYANTHA ROSES   Cultivars marked with a dagger (†) are polyanthas.

Rose, year of introduction, awards	ARS rating*	Flower color	Flower description and blooming habits	Foliage, growth habits, and cultural tips
Koricole (Nicole), (1985)	9.0	White with deep raspberry edges	Large, double, cupped, with golden stamens; in large clusters.	Large, dark green, glossy; upright, medium tall; vigorous, disease resistant, hardy edges.
Little Darling (1956), Portland Gold Medal, 1958; David Fuerstenberg Prize, 1964	8.6	Yellow suffused with salmon pink	2½" double, well formed, small to medium clusters; spicy fragrance.	Dark green, glossy, leathery; very vigorous; spreading and tall.
†Margo Koster (Sunbeam), (1931)	8.3	Salmon	1"–2" double; slight fragrance; free blooming.	Glossy; compact, to 24"; disease resistant; good for borders, containers.
Marina (1974), AARS 1981	7.7	Orange with yellow base	2½"–3" double; slightly fragrant; good cut.	Glossy, dark green; bushy, compact, medium height; disease resistant.
Nana Mouskouri (1975)	8.1	White	4" double, well formed; small clusters; fragrant.	Large, dark green, semiglossy; vigorous; short to medium size.
Pleasure (1990), AARS 1990	7.9	Coral pink with salmon	4" double; abundant; slightly fragrant.	Medium green; upright, 3'–4', extremely vigorous; resistant to rust and powdery mildew; hardy.
Redgold (Rouge et Or), (1971), AARS 1971	7.4	Golden yellow edged deep pink	2"–3" double; slight scent; abundant and continual; long lasting.	Glossy, light green; tall, vigorous, 2'–3'; disease resistant; allergic to some sprays.
Sexy Rexy (1984)	9.0	Medium to light pink	2½"–3½" double; borne in large clusters; slight fragrance; profuse.	Light green, glossy; vigorous, bushy; very disease resistant; good for hedges.

Sun Flare

Simplicity

Redgold

Showbiz

Pleasure

FLORIBUNDA AND POLYANTHA ROSES   Cultivars marked with a dagger (†) are polyanthas.

Rose, year of introduction, awards	ARS rating*	Flower color	Flower description and blooming habits	Foliage, growth habits, and cultural tips
Showbiz (1981), AARS 1985	8.6	Bright medium red	Medium-sized double; loosely formed; borne in large clusters; no fragrance.	Medium green, semiglossy; low, bushy; disease resistant; good for hedges.
Simplicity (1979)	8.1	Light to medium pink	3"–4" semidouble; borne in large clusters.	Medium green; bushy, medium height; disease resistant; hardy; excellent as a hedge or border.
Summer Fashion (1985)	8.0	Pale yellow, edged pink; pink spreads with age	Large double; borne singly or in small clusters; fragrant.	Medium green, semiglossy; short to medium height, bushy, slightly spreading.
Sun Flare (1983), AARS 1983	8.1	Lemon yellow	3" semidouble; mild licorice fragrance; free blooming.	Glossy, deep green; low, round, somewhat spreading; disease resistant.
Sunsprite (1977), James Alexander Gamble Rose Fragrance Medal 1979	8.7	Deep golden yellow	3" double; borne in clusters of 5 or more; very fragrant.	Light green; upright, short to medium height; disease resistant; tender.
Sweet Inspiration (1993), AARS 1993	N.R.	Medium pink with cream base	Large, double; in large clusters.	Medium sized, matte green; upright, bushy, medium height.
†The Fairy (1932)	8.7	Pink	1½" double; slight fragrance; profuse; large clusters.	Glossy, dark green, fernlike; short, compact, to 2½'; very disease resistant; hardy; good for low hedges.

Love

Aquarius

Solitude

GRANDIFLORA ROSES

Rose, year of introduction, awards	ARS rating*	Flower color	Flower description and blooming habits	Foliage, growth habits, and cultural tips
Aquarius (1971), AARS 1971	8.0	Medium pink blend	4" double; moderate fragrance; free blooming.	Leathery; medium to tall, upright; very disease resistant; hardy.
Caribbean (1994), AARS 1994	N.R.	Orange with yellow reverse	4" very double.	Bright green, semiglossy; medium height.
Gold Medal (1982)	8.8	Deep yellow	3½"–4" double; little fragrance; buds edged orange-red on deep gold; abundant.	Glossy, deep green; tall, vigorous; remarkably hardy.
Love (1980), AARS 1980	7.1	Scarlet with silvery white reverse	3½" double; spicy fragrance; free blooming; good cut.	Medium green; broad, full, upright; resistant to powdery mildew.
Olé (1964)	7.3	Red-orange	3½" double; moderate scent; ruffled, camellialike petals; prolific; good cut.	Attractive, deep green, glossy; short, bushy, to 3'; disease resistant; tender.
Pink Parfait (1960), AARS 1961	8.2	Medium pink	3½" double; slight fragrance; abundant; good cut.	Bright green, glossy; vigorous, heavily branched; disease resistant.
Prima Donna (1983), AARS 1988	7.5	Deep fuchsia pink	4" double; well formed; slight fragrance.	Medium green, semiglossy; bushy, spreading, medium height; hardy; susceptible to powdery mildew and blackspot.

Caribbean

Queen Elizabeth

Prominent

Sonia

GRANDIFLORA ROSES

Rose, year of introduction, awards	ARS rating*	Flower color	Flower description and blooming habits	Foliage, growth habits, and cultural tips
Prominent (1971), AARS 1977	7.2	Hot orange	3" double; light, fruity fragrance; continuous blooms; colorfast; good cut.	Glossy, leathery; medium height; disease resistant.
Queen Elizabeth (1954), AARS 1955, ARS Gold Medal Certificate 1960	9.0	Carmine, rose, and pale pink	3½"–4" double; moderate fragrance; profuse, continual.	Dark green, glossy; very vigorous and tall, 4'–6'; very hardy; very disease resistant; good for hedges; a classic, deservedly so.
Scarlet Knight (Samourai), (1966), AARS 1968	7.0	Scarlet	4"–5" double; slight fragrance; velvety petals; good color retention; free blooming; good cut.	Leathery; upright, bushy, to over 4'; thorny; disease resistant.
Shining Hour (1990), AARS 1991	7.6	Dark yellow	Medium size, double, cupped; in sprays of 3–5; fruity fragrance.	Large, dark green, semiglossy; upright, medium height.
Solitude (1992), AARS 1993	N.R.	Orange and yellow bicolor	Medium sized, double; in large clusters.	Medium, bright green, semiglossy; bushy, medium height.
Sonia (1974)	8.1	Pink to coral to yellow	4" double; spicy fragrance; profuse, long lasting; good cut.	Deep green; bushy, medium height; disease resistant.
Tournament of Roses (1988), AARS 1988	8.0	Coral pink, lightens faster on top than reverse	4" double; unusual bicolor effect; very prolific; slightly fragrant.	Dark green, glossy; upright, vigorous, medium height; hardy.

Fred Loads

Climbing Cécile Brünner

New Dawn

Altissimo

America

CLIMBERS

Rose, year of introduction, awards	ARS rating*	Flower color	Flower description and blooming habits	Foliage, growth habits, and cultural tips
Altissimo (Altus), (1966)	9.3	Blood red	7 petals, cupped to flat; in large clusters; good repeat bloom.	Dark green; very tall, vigorous.
America (1976), large-flowered climber, AARS 1976	8.8	Coral pink	4"–5" double; spicy, carnationlike fragrance; hybrid tea flowers; profuse all season.	Dark green, leathery; moderately tall; disease resistant; hardy; easy to grow; good as pillar rose.
Blaze (1932), large-flowered climber	7.4	Scarlet	2"–3" semidouble; slight fragrance; borne in large clusters; prolific in spring, with smaller blooms throughout summer and fall.	Dark green, leathery; fast growing, 12'–15'; hardy; widely planted, easy to grow; susceptible to powdery mildew.
City of York (1945), ARS Gold Medal 1950	8.4	Creamy white	Large, semidouble, cupped; in clusters of 7–15; fragrant; spring bloom only.	Dark green, glossy, leathery; very vigorous and hardy.
Clair Matin (1960), Gold Medal, Bagatelle, 1960	8.8	Medium pink	2"–3" semidouble, cupped to flat; in large clusters; repeats.	Dark, leathery; vigorous, 10'–12' high.
Climbing Cécile Brünner (1894), climbing polyantha	8.0	Bright pink on yellow	1"–1½" double; moderate fragrance; strong blooms in spring and fall.	Dark green; vigorous, to 20'; good for trellises and arbors.
Don Juan (1958), large-flowered climber	8.2	Dark red	4"–5" double; heavy fragrance; profuse throughout season; long lasting; good cut.	Dark green, glossy, leathery; vigorous, upright, to 8'; fairly hardy; disease resistant; excellent as pillar rose.
Elegance (1937), large-flowered climber	6.9	Medium yellow	6" very double; fragrant; long, strong stems; somewhat recurrent.	Glossy; very vigorous, 10'–12'; very hardy.
Fred Loads (1968), climbing floribunda	8.3	Vermilion-orange	3" single; borne in clusters; fragrant; repeats.	Glossy; vigorous, tall; performs well in most climates.
Galway Bay (1966)	8.0	Salmon pink	3½" semidouble; small to medium clusters.	Dark green; tall and vigorous.

Blaze

Handel

Golden Showers

CLIMBERS

Rose, year of introduction, awards	ARS rating*	Flower color	Flower description and blooming habits	Foliage, growth habits, and cultural tips
Golden Showers (1956), large-flowered climber, AARS 1957	7.4	Daffodil yellow	4" double; moderate fragrance; long stems; profuse, continual.	Dark, glossy; vigorous, 8'–12'; excellent as pillar rose.
Handel (1965), large-flowered climber	8.2	Cream edged with rosy red	3½" double; pleasant, light scent; prolific throughout season.	Dark green, glossy; vigorous, 12'–14'; will tolerate some shade; good for posts, walls, fences, small structures.
Jeanne Lajoie (1975), climbing miniature, ARS Award of Excellence 1977	9.2	Medium pink	1" double; slightly fragrant; prolific.	Small, dark green, glossy leaves; upright, bushy; one of the few true climbing miniatures.
Joseph's Coat (1964), large-flowered climber	7.6	Yellow and red	3" double; slight fragrance; very free blooming; a riot of bright color all season long.	Dark green, glossy; vigorous; somewhat tender; prone to powdery mildew; can be planted as a shrub, pillar, or climber.
New Dawn (1930), large-flowered climber	7.9	Pink	2"–3" double; fragrant; profuse; continual.	Glossy, dark green; vigorous, 12'–20'; somewhat hardy; disease resistant; also makes a good ground cover.
Paul's Scarlet Climber (1916), large-flowered climber	7.0	Scarlet shaded to crimson	2"–3" semidouble; slight scent; many large clusters; one flowering in spring.	Dark, leathery; vigorous, 10'–15'; very hardy; susceptible to powdery mildew.
Pelé (1979), climbing hybrid tea	6.8	White	Large double; borne in clusters of 1–3; fruity fragrance; repeats.	Medium green; upright; develops long canes and climbs in warm-winter areas, grows like a bush elsewhere.
Royal Sunset (1960), large-flowered climber	8.4	Apricot fading to peach	4½" double; slight scent; good bloom all season.	Glossy, broad, coppery green; vigorous, to 10'; disease resistant; good on posts, fences, or small structures.
White Dawn (1949), large-flowered climber	7.0	Pure white	2"–3" double; fragrant; gardenialike flowers in clusters; continual, but best displays in spring and fall.	Dark green, glossy; vigorous, 10'–12'; disease resistant; quite hardy.

Loving Touch

Debut

MINIATURE ROSES

Rose, year of introduction, awards	ARS rating*	Flower color	Flower description and blooming habits	Foliage, growth habits, and cultural tips
Baby Darling (1964)	7.5	Orange to orange-pink	1¾" double; slight fragrance.	Medium green leaves; moderately compact, 12"–14"; relatively tender.
Baby Eclipse (1984), ARS Award of Excellence 1984	6.7	Medium yellow	Small semidouble; slight fragrance.	Small, medium green leaves; bushy, spreading, can reach 5' × 5' in warm-winter areas.
Beauty Secret (1965), ARS Award of Excellence 1975	8.4	Cardinal red	1"–1½" semidouble; very fragrant; hybrid tea buds; abundant; good cut.	Glossy, leathery; moderately compact, 8"–10"; very hardy; good in semishade; easy to grow.
Black Jade (1985), ARS Award of Excellence 1985	8.3	Scarlet overlaid with black	Small double; black buds open to dark red; no fragrance.	Medium-sized, dark, semiglossy leaves; bushy; hardy.
Child's Play (1991), AARS 1993, ARS Award of Excellence 1993	N.R.	White and pink bicolor	Medium-sized semidouble, high centered; borne singly and in sprays of 3 or more; sweet fragrance.	Medium, dark green; upright, medium height.
Cinderella (1953)	8.2	White with pale pink edging	¾"–1" double; spicy fragrance; prolific; good cut.	Glossy; compact, 12"–15"; thornless; disease resistant; easy to grow.
Cupcake (1981), ARS Award of Excellence 1983	8.5	Pink	1½" double; well-formed hybrid tea buds; profuse; no fragrance.	Dark green; compact.
Debut (1989), AARS 1989	7.4	Deep crimson, creamy white at base	1½" double; good stem length for cutting; no fragrance; abundant and continuous.	Rich, glossy green; vigorous, 12"–18"; fairly disease resistant; good landscaping plant.
Dreamglo (1978)	8.5	Red and white blend	1½" double; long, pointed hybrid tea buds; long lasting.	Glossy; moderately compact, vigorous; healthy.
Gourmet Popcorn (1986)	8.4	Pure white with yellow stamens	1½" semidouble; borne in clusters; honey fragrance; constantly repeats.	Dark green, glossy; extremely vigorous; upright to 3'; disease resistant.
Holy Toledo (1978), ARS Award of Excellence 1980	7.9	Apricot orange with yellow-orange center and reverse	2" double; slight fragrance; prolific, long lasting.	Deep green, glossy; vigorous, to 20".

Pride 'n Joy

Luis Desamero

Black Jade

Cupcake

Dreamglo

MINIATURE ROSES

Rose, year of introduction, awards	ARS rating*	Flower color	Flower description and blooming habits	Foliage, growth habits, and cultural tips
Jean Kenneally (1984), ARS Award of Excellence 1986	9.7	Pale to medium apricot	Small double; hybrid tea form; slight fragrance; heavy bloomer.	Medium-sized, medium green, semiglossy leaves; upright, bushy, tall for a miniature; hardy.
Jennifer (1985), ARS Award of Excellence 1985	8.1	Light pink, white reverse	1½" double; hybrid tea form; very fragrant.	Dark green, semiglossy; bushy, spreading.
Kingig (Giggles), (1987)	9.0	Light pink, with reverse of dark pink fading to creamy white	Medium-sized semidouble, high centered; borne singly or in small clusters.	Bright green; upright, tall.
Kristin (1992), ARS Award of Excellence 1993	N.R.	White edged with red	Medium-sized very double, high centered; borne singly or in small clusters.	Large, dark green, semiglossy; upright, bushy, medium height.
Little Jackie (1982), ARS Award of Excellence 1984	8.6	Light orange-red, yellow reverse	Small double; very fragrant.	Medium green, semiglossy; vigorous; prone to powdery mildew.
Loving Touch (1982), ARS Award of Excellence 1985	8.6	Pale apricot	Medium-sized double; almost as big as a floribunda in cool weather, smaller in hot weather; hybrid tea form; usually borne singly; slight fragrance.	Medium green, semiglossy; bushy, spreading.
Luis Desamero (1989)	7.7	Pale yellow	Medium-sized, double, high centered; borne singly and in sprays of 3–5; fruity fragrance.	Medium, bright green, semiglossy; upright, bushy, tall.
Magic Carrousel (1972), ARS Award of Excellence 1975	9.0	White with red edges	Small double; hybrid tea form; borne singly and in small clusters; slight fragrance.	Small, glossy, leathery leaves; vigorous, bushy; easy to grow.
Mary Marshall (1970), ARS Award of Excellence 1975	8.0	Orange with yellow base	1¾" double; moderate fragrance; profuse all season; good cut.	Leathery, medium green; moderately compact, 10"–12"; disease resistant.
Minnie Pearl (1982)	9.4	Light pink	Small double; hybrid tea form; slight fragrance; in constant bloom.	Small, medium green, semiglossy leaves; very vigorous, upright.

New Beginning

Peaches 'n Cream

Party Girl

MINIATURE ROSES

Rose, year of introduction, awards	ARS rating*	Flower color	Flower description and blooming habits	Foliage, growth habits, and cultural tips
My Sunshine (1986)	8.7	Medium yellow, aging to soft orange	Medium sized; borne singly and in small sprays; fragrant.	Bright green, semiglossy; upright, bushy, medium height.
New Beginning (1989), AARS 1989	7.1	Orange-red with golden reverse and base	1¼" double; no fragrance but spectacular color; among first minis to bloom in spring; prolific.	Medium green; vigorous, 18"–20"; very disease resistant; good border.
Over the Rainbow (1972), ARS Award of Excellence 1975	8.3	Red and yellow	1¾" double; little fragrance; abundant.	Leathery, medium green; vigorous, bushy, 12"–14"; disease resistant.
Pacesetter (1979), ARS Award of Excellence 1981		White	1½" very double, high centered; fragrant.	Dark green; vigorous, compact growth.
Party Girl (1979), ARS Award of Excellence 1981	9.0	Soft apricot yellow	1" double; spicy fragrance.	Medium green; compact, bushy; hardy.
Peaches 'n Cream (1976), ARS Award of Excellence 1977	8.4	Light peach, muted with white	1" double; borne singly and in clusters; slight fragrance.	Dark green; upright, spreading, very vigorous; hardy.
Pierrine (1988)	9.4	Pink	Medium-sized, very double, high centered; borne mostly singly; damask fragrance.	Bright green, semiglossy; upright, medium height.
Pride 'n Joy (1991), AARS 1992	N.R.	Bright orange with reverse of orange and cream fading to salmon pink	Medium, double; fruity fragrance.	Medium sized, dark green, semiglossy; bushy, spreading, medium height.
Puppy Love (1978), ARS Award of Excellence 1979	7.4	Orange, pink, and coral blend	1½"–1¾" double; slight fragrance; borne singly on long stems; free blooming; good cut.	Small, glossy leaves; compact, shapely, to 16".

Rise 'n Shine

Puppy Love

Rainbow's End

Valerie Jeanne

MINIATURE ROSES

Rose, year of introduction, awards	ARS rating*	Flower color	Flower description and blooming habits	Foliage, growth habits, and cultural tips
Rainbow's End (1984), ARS Award of Excellence 1986	9.0	Deep yellow with red edges, ages red all over	Small double; hybrid tea form; prolific and constant; no fragrance.	Small, dark green, glossy leaves; upright, bushy, vigorous; hardy; easy to grow.
Red Cascade (1976), ARS Award of Excellence 1976	7.2	Deep red	1" double; cupped; slightly fragrant; very prolific; entirely covered in blooms.	Small, leathery leaves; prostrate, bushy; good in hanging baskets and as spreading ground cover.
Rise 'n Shine (1977), ARS Award of Excellence 1978	9.1	Medium yellow	2"–2¼" double; little fragrance; abundant and continuous; good cut.	Small, glossy, deep green leaves, good foil for the blossoms; moderately compact, vigorous, 12"–14"; disease resistant; easy to grow.
Simplex (1961)	8.2	Apricot bud opens white with gold stamens	1½" single; borne in small clusters; slight fragrance.	Leathery; vigorous, bushy, 12"–14".
Snow Bride (1982), ARS Award of Excellence 1983	9.3	White	1¾" single; little fragrance; hybrid tea buds; large clusters.	Glossy; moderately compact; easy to grow.
Starina (1965)	9.0	Scarlet-orange	1½"–2" double; no fragrance; outstanding bud and flower form; abundant, continuous; good cut.	Small, glossy; vigorous, moderately compact, 15"–18"; relatively tender.
Toy Clown (1966), ARS Award of Excellence 1975	8.1	White with red edges	Small semidouble; hybrid tea form.	Small, leathery, deep green leaves; bushy, vigorous, medium height; hardy.
Valerie Jeanne (1980), ARS Award of Excellence 1983	7.6	Deep magenta to pink	1½"–2" double; in clusters of 1–20; slight fragrance.	Very glossy; upright, vigorous.
Winsome (1985), ARS Award of Excellence 1985	8.5	Plum-mauve	1½"–2" double; hybrid tea form; borne singly and in clusters; no fragrance but unusual color.	Dark, semiglossy; bushy, upright, vigorous; disease resistant.

ROSES FOR SPECIAL PURPOSES

On the following pages are lists of roses that are particularly recommended for fragrance, cut flowers, and other special purposes. All of the roses discussed in this book are also listed by color. For more information on each variety, refer to the charts beginning on page 72.

Key to Abbreviations

Cl   Climber
F   Floribunda
Gr   Grandiflora
HT   Hybrid Tea
M   Miniature
MS   Modern Shrub
OGR   Old Garden Rose
Pol   Polyantha
Sp   Species

ROSES FOR SCREENS

Altissimo (Cl)
America (Cl)
Blaze (Cl)
City of York (Cl)
Clair Matin (Cl)
Communis (OGR)
Constance Spry (MS)
Crested Moss (OGR)
Don Juan (Cl)
Dortmund (MS)
Félicité et Perpétué (OGR)
Folklore (HT)
Fred Loads (Cl)
Frühlingsgold (OGR)
Galway Bay (Cl)
Golden Showers (Cl)
Harison's Yellow (OGR)
Kathleen (MS)
Mermaid (OGR)
Nevada (MS)
New Dawn (Cl)
Paul's Scarlet Climber (Cl)
Rosa banksiae (Sp)
Rosa eglanteria (Sp)
Rosa foetida bicolor (Sp)
Rosa hugonis (Sp)
Rosa laevigata (Sp)
Rosa moyesii (Sp)
Salet (OGR)
Sombreuil (OGR)

Floribunda 'Anabell'

Sparrieshoop (MS)
Stanwell Perpetual (OGR)
Sunny June (MS)

ROSES FOR HEDGES

All That Jazz (MS)
Blanc Double de Coubert (MS)
Carefree Wonder (MS)
Dicky (F)
Duet (HT)
Europeana (F)
Eyepaint (F)
Frau Dagmar Hartopp (MS)
Golden Wings (MS)
H. C. Andersen (F)
Iceberg (F)
Madame Hardy (OGR)
Meidomonac (Bonica '82) (MS)
Old Blush (OGR)
Pink Grootendorst (MS)
Queen Elizabeth (Gr)
Rosa rugosa (Sp)
Sexy Rexy (F)
Showbiz (F)
Simplicity (F)
The Fairy (Pol)

ROSES FOR GROUND COVERS

Dortmund (MS)
Félicité et Perpétué (OGR)
Ferdinand Pichard (OGR)

New Dawn (Cl)
Red Cascade (M)
Rosa laevigata (Sp)
Rosa spinosissima (Sp)
Rosa wichuraiana (Sp)

ROSES BY COLOR

Red Roses

Altissimo (CL)
Beauty Secret (M)
Black Jade (M)
Blaze (Cl)
Chrysler Imperial (HT)
Crimson Glory (HT)
Don Juan (Cl)
Dortmund (MS)
Dublin (HT)
Esperanza (F)
Europeana (F)
Eyepaint (F)
Ferdinand Pichard (OGR)
Général Jacqueminot (OGR)
H. C. Andersen (F)
Korlingo (F)
Loving Memory (HT)
Mister Lincoln (HT)
Olympiad (HT)
Papa Meilland (HT)
Paul's Scarlet Climber (Cl)
Precious Platinum (HT)
Red Cascade (M)

Rosa moyesii (Sp)
Scarlet Knight (Gr)
Showbiz (F)
Swarthmore (HT)
Trojan Victory (HT)
Uncle Joe (HT)

Pink Roses
America (Cl)
Apothecary's Rose (OGR)
Aquarius (Gr)
Autumn Damask (OGR)
Baronne Prévost (OGR)
Betty Prior (F)
Bewitched (HT)
Bride's Dream (HT)
Brigadoon (HT)
Captain Harry Stebbings (HT)
Carefree Wonder (MS)
Cécile Brünner (Pol)
Celestial (OGR)
Century Two (HT)
Charlotte Armstrong (HT)
Cherish (F)
China Doll (Pol)
Clair Matin (Cl)
Climbing Cécile Brünner (Cl)
Communis (OGR)
Complicata (OGR)
Comte de Chambord (OGR)
Confidence (HT)

Hybrid tea 'Paradise'

Constance Spry (MS)
Crested Moss (OGR)
Cupcake (M)
Dainty Bess (HT)
Duchesse de Brabant (OGR)
Duet (HT)
Electron (HT)
Elizabeth Taylor (HT)
Fantin-Latour (OGR)
First Prize (HT)

Frau Dagmar Hartopp (MS)
Galway Bay (Cl)
Gene Boerner (F)
Great Scott (HT)
Hermosa (OGR)
Honorine de Brabant (OGR)
Jeanne Lajoie (Cl)
Jennifer (M)
Kathleen (MS)
Keepsake (HT)
Kingig (M)
Königin von Dänemark (OGR)
La Reine Victoria (OGR)
Maman Cochet (OGR)
Marijke Koopman (HT)
Marquise Boccella (OGR)
Meidomonac (Bonica '82) (MS)
Minnie Pearl (M)
Miss All-American Beauty (HT)
New Dawn (Cl)
Old Blush (OGR)
Pierrine (M)
Perfume Delight (HT)
Pink Grootendorst (MS)
Pink Parfait (Gr)
Pleasure (F)
Prima Donna (Gr)
Queen Elizabeth (Gr)
Rosa eglanteria (Sp)
Rosa glauca (Sp)
Rosa virginiana (Sp)
Rose de Meaux (OGR)

Grandiflora 'Gold Medal'

Royal Highness (HT)
Salet (OGR)
Secret (HT)
Sexy Rexy (F)
Sheer Elegance (HT)
Simplicity (F)
Sparrieshoop (MS)
Sweet Inspiration (F)
The Fairy (Pol)
Tiffany (HT)
Touch of Class (HT)
Tournament of Roses (Gr)
Valerie Jeanne (M)
York and Lancaster (OGR)

Lavender to Purple Roses
Angel Face (F)
Intrigue (F)
Lady X (HT)
Madame Violebrut (HT)
Paradise (HT)
Reine des Violettes (OGR)
Rosa rugosa (Sp)
Silverado (HT)
Superb Tuscan (OGR)
Winsome (M)
Wise Portia (MS)

Yellow Roses
Baby Eclipse (M)
Elegance (Cl)
Elina (HT)
Frühlingsgold (OGR)
Gold Medal (Gr)
Golden Showers (Cl)
Golden Wings (MS)
Harison's Yellow (OGR)
Helmut Schmidt (HT)
Little Darling (F)
Luis Desamero (M)
Maid of Honour (HT)
Mermaid (OGR)
Midas Touch (HT)
My Sunshine (M)
Oregold (HT)
Party Girl (M)
Rise 'n Shine (M)
Rosa banksiae (Sp)
Rosa foetida persiana (Sp)
Rosa hugonis (Sp)
Shining Hour (Gr)
Sun Flare (F)
Sunny June (MS)

Climber 'City of York'

Hybrid tea 'Die Welt'

Floribunda 'Orangeade'

Old garden rose 'Salet'

Lamarque (OGR)
Madame Hardy (OGR)
Miyabi (HT)
Nana Mouskouri (F)
Nevada (MS)
Pacesetter (M)
Pascali (HT)
Pelé (Cl)
Pristine (HT)
Rosa banksiae (Sp)
Rosa laevigata (Sp)
Rosa spinosissima (Sp)
Rosa wichuraiana (Sp)
Sheer Bliss (HT)
Simplex (M)
Snow Bride (M)
Sombreuil (OGR)
Souvenir de la Malmaison (OGR)
Stanwell Perpetual (OGR)
Suffolk (HT)
Summer Fashion (F)
White Dawn (Cl)
White Masterpiece (HT)
White Success (HT)

Sunsprite (F)
Sutter's Gold (HT)

Apricot Roses
Apricot Nectar (F)
Baby Darling (M)
Brandy (HT)
Buff Beauty (MS)
Jean Kenneally (M)
Loving Touch (M)
Royal Sunset (Cl)

Orange-Red and Orange to Gold Roses
All That Jazz (MS)
Anabell (F)
Caribbean (Gr)
Cary Grant (HT)
Dicky (F)
Dolly Parton (HT)
First Edition (F)
Folklore (HT)
Fragrant Cloud (HT)
Fred Loads (Cl)
Impatient (F)
Little Jackie (M)
Margo Koster (Pol)
Marina (F)

Mary Marshall (M)
New Beginning (M)
Olé (Gr)
Pride 'n Joy (M)
Prominent (Gr)
Puppy Love (M)
Solitude (Gr)
Starina (M)
Tropicana (HT)

White to Cream Roses
Blanc Double de Coubert (MS)
Child's Play (M)
Cinderella (M)
City of York (Cl)
Class Act (F)
Fair Bianca (MS)
Félicité et Perpétué (OGR)
Frau Karl Druschki (OGR)
French Lace (F)
Garden Party (HT)
Gourmet Popcorn (M)
Great Maiden's Blush (OGR)
Honor (HT)
Iceberg (F)
Ivory Fashion (F)
Koricole (F)
Kristin (M)

Bicolor and Multicolor Roses
Chicago Peace (HT)
Color Magic (HT)
Debut (M)
Double Delight (HT)
Dreamglo (M)
Granada (HT)
Handel (Cl)
Holy Toledo (M)
Joseph's Coat (Cl)
Love (Gr)
Magic Carrousel (M)
Mikado (HT)
Mon Cheri (HT)
Osiria (HT)
Over the Rainbow (M)
Peace (HT)
Peaches 'n Cream (M)
Perfect Moment (HT)
Rainbow's End (M)
Redgold (F)
Rio Samba (HT)
Rosa foetida bicolor (Sp)
Rosa Mundi (OGR)
Sonia (Gr)
Toy Clown (M)
Voodoo (HT)

ESPECIALLY FRAGRANT ROSES

Angel Face (F)
Apothecary's Rose (OGR)
Autumn Damask (OGR)
Beauty Secret (M)
Bewitched (HT)
Blanc Double de Coubert (MS)
Bride's Dream (HT)
Captain Harry Stebbings (HT)
Child's Play (M)
Chrysler Imperial (HT) *
City of York (Cl)
Communis (OGR)
Confidence (HT)
Crimson Glory (HT) *
Dolly Parton (HT)
Don Juan (Cl)
Double Delight (HT) *
Dublin (HT)
Duchesse de Brabant (OGR)
Folklore (HT)
Fragrant Cloud (HT) *
Général Jacqueminot (OGR)
Granada (HT) *

Honorine de Brabant (OGR)
Iceberg (F)
Intrigue (F)
Keepsake (HT)
Königin von Dänemark (OGR)
Little Darling (F)
Madame Hardy (OGR)
Nana Mouskouri (F)
Pacesetter (M)
Papa Meilland (HT)*
Perfume Delight (HT)
Pierrine (M)
Pride 'n Joy (M)
Rosa laevigata (Sp)
Rosa rugosa (Sp)
Salet (OGR)
Secret (HT)
Sombreuil (OGR)
Sonia (Gr)
Sunsprite (F) *
Sutter's Gold (HT) *
Tiffany (HT) *
* Winners of the James Alexander Gamble Rose Fragrance Medal (see page 33)

LONG-LASTING CUT ROSES

Anabell (F)
Bewitched (HT)
Brigadoon (HT)
Captain Harry Stebbings (HT)
Cary Grant (HT)
Century Two (HT)
Chrysler Imperial (HT)
Cupcake (M)
Dicky (F)
Dolly Parton (HT)
Double Delight (HT)
Dublin (HT)
Elina (HT)
Elizabeth Taylor (HT)
First Edition (F)
First Prize (HT)
Folklore (HT)
Garden Party (HT)
Great Scott (HT)
Jean Kenneally (M)
Korlingo (HT)
Kristin (M)
Lady X (HT)
Little Darling (F)
Love (Gr)
Maid of Honour (HT)
Marina (F)
Mister Lincoln (HT)
Mon Cheri (HT)
Paradise (HT)
Pascali (HT)
Peace (HT)
Peaches 'n Cream (M)
Pierrine (M)
Precious Platinum (HT)
Prominent (Gr)
Royal Highness (HT)
Sheer Elegance (HT)
Silverado (HT)
Sonia (Gr)
Starina (M)
Suffolk (HT)
Swarthmore (HT)
Tiffany (HT)
Touch of Class (HT)
Trojan Victory (HT)
Tropicana (HT)
Uncle Joe (HT)
White Masterpiece (HT)

Floribunda 'Impatient'

HARDIEST MODERN ROSES**

Bewitched (HT)
Black Jade (M)
Blanc Double de Coubert (MS)
Captain Harry Stebbings (HT)
Carefree Wonder (MS)
City of York (Cl)
Crimson Glory (HT)
Dicky (F)
Dortmund (MS)
Dublin (HT)
Elina (HT)
Europeana (F)
Eyepaint (F)
Folklore (HT)
Frau Dagmar Hartopp (MS)
Garden Party (HT)
Gold Medal (Gr)
Golden Wings (MS)
Great Scott (HT)
H. C. Andersen (F)
Iceberg (F)
Jean Kenneally (M)
Jennifer (M)
Kathleen (MS)
Koricole (F)
Lady X (HT)
Little Darling (F)
Loving Memory (HT)
Maid of Honour (HT)
Marijke Koopman (HT)
Meidomonac (Bonica '82) (MS)
Nevada (MS)
Pacesetter (M)
Pink Grootendoorst (MS)
Precious Platinum (HT)
Suffolk (HT)
Swarthmore (HT)
Trojan Victory (HT)
Uncle Joe (HT)

** Most species roses and old garden roses, except teas, are extremely hardy.

MOST DISEASE-RESISTANT ROSES

Bride's Dream (HT)
Brigadoon (HT)
Carefree Wonder (MS)
City of York (Cl)
Confidence (HT)
Dicky (F)

Floribunda 'Summer Fashion'

Dortmund (MS)
Dublin (HT)
Elina (HT)
First Prize (HT)
Folklore (HT)
Gold Medal (Gr)
Great Scott (HT)
H. C. Andersen (F)
Keepsake (HT)
Koricole (F)
Korlingo (HT)
Maid of Honour (HT)
Marijke Koopman (HT)
Meidomonac (Bonica '82) (MS)
Miyabi (HT)
Olympiad (HT)
Osiria (HT)
Pink Parfait (Gr)
Precious Platinum (HT)
Pristine (HT)
Sheer Elegance (HT)
Suffolk (HT)
Trojan Victory (HT)
Uncle Joe (HT)
White Success (HT)

EASIEST-TO-GROW ROSES

Beauty Secret (M)
Betty Prior (F)
Bewitched (HT)
Blaze (Cl)
Cherish (F)
City of York (Cl)
Dicky (F)

Dortmund (MS)
Dublin (HT)
Duet (HT)
Elina (HT)
Europeana (F)
First Prize (HT)
Folklore (HT)
Fragrant Cloud (HT)
Garden Party (HT)
Gold Medal (Gr)
Great Scott (HT)
H. C. Andersen (F)
Harison's Yellow (OGR)
Iceberg (F)
Koricole (F)
Korlingo (HT)
Kristin (M)
Little Darling (F)
Magic Carrousel (M)
Maid of Honour (HT)
Meidomonac (Bonica '82) (MS)
Minnie Pearl (M)
Mister Lincoln (HT)
Miyabi (HT)
Pacesetter (M)
Pristine (HT)
Queen Elizabeth (Gr)
Rainbow's End (M)
Rise 'n Shine (M)
Rosa eglanteria (Sp)
Snow Bride (M)
Suffolk (HT)
Trojan Victory (HT)
Tropicana (HT)

Sources

It's always better to purchase plants and materials from a local nursery, where you can see items before buying them and where you don't have to pay shipping costs. But if you can't find the roses you want locally, here are some mail-order sources. Only rose specialists are included here; many general nurseries also carry a wide line of roses.

The Antique Rose Emporium
Route 5, Box 143
Brenham, TX 77833
(800) 441-0002; fax: (409) 836-0928
Old garden roses

Bridges Roses
Lawndale, NC 28090
(704) 538-9412
Miniatures

Carroll Gardens, Inc.
Box 310
Westminster, MD 21157
(800) 638-6334
General nursery with a good selection of roses

Greenmantle Nursery
3010 Ettersburg Road
Garberville, CA 95542
(707) 986-7504
Old garden and species roses

Heirloom Old Garden Roses
24062 NE Riverside Drive
St. Paul, OR 97137
(503) 538-1576; fax: (503) 538-5902
Old garden roses and David Austin varieties

Heritage Rosarium
211 Haviland Mill Road
Brookeville, MD 20833
(301) 774-2806
Old garden, climbing, and species roses

Heritage Rose Gardens
16831 Mitchell Creek Drive
Fort Bragg, CA 95437
(707) 984-6959
Old garden roses

Historical Roses
1657 West Jackson Street
Painesville, OH 44077
(216) 357-7270
Old garden roses

Inter-State Nurseries
1800 Hamilton Road
Bloomington, IL 61704
(309) 663-9551
Modern roses

Jackson & Perkins Co.
1 Rose Lane
Medford, OR 97501
(800) 292-4769
Modern roses

Justice Miniature Roses
5947 Southwest Kahle Road
Wilsonville, OR 97070
(503) 682-2370

Lowe's Own-Root Roses
6 Sheffield Road
Nashua, NH 03062-3028
(603) 888-2214
Old garden roses, species, and modern shrubs, grown on their own roots

McDaniel's Miniature Roses
7523 Zemco Street
Lemon Grove, CA 92045
(619) 469-4669

Mendocino Heirloom Roses
Box 670
Mendocino, CA 95460
Old garden roses on their own roots

Miniature Plant Kingdom
4125 Harrison Grade Road
Sebastopol, CA 95472
Miniature roses

Nor'East Miniature Roses
Box 473
Ontario, CA 91762

Nor'East Miniature Roses
58 Hammond Street
Rowley, MA 01969

Oregon Miniature Roses, Inc.
8285 Southwest 185th Avenue
Beaverton, OR 97007
(503) 649-4482

Carl Pallek and Sons Nurseries
Box 137
Virgil, Ontario L0S 1T0 Canada
(905)468-7262
Wide variety of roses. Ships to Canada only

Pickering Nurseries, Inc.
670 Kingston Road
Pickering, Ontario L1V 1A6
Canada
(905) 839-2111; fax: (905) 839-4807
Wide variety of roses

Pixie Treasures Miniature Roses
4121 Prospect Avenue
Yorba Linda, CA 92686
(714) 993-6780

Rose Acres
6641 Crystal Boulevard
Diamond Springs, CA 95619
(916) 626-1722
Wide variety of roses, many on their own roots

The Mini Rose Garden
Box 203
Cross Hill, SC 29332
(800) 996-4647; fax: (803) 998-4947

Rosehill Farm
Box 188
Gregg Neck Road
Galena, MD 21635
(301) 648-5538
Miniatures

Roses by Fred Edmunds, Inc.
6235 Southwest Kahle Road
Wilsonville, OR 97070
(503) 682-1476; fax: (503) 682-1275
Modern roses

Roses of Yesterday and Today
802 Brown's Valley Road
Watsonville, CA 95076
(408) 724-3537
Old garden and modern roses

Royall River Roses
Forevergreen Farm
70 New Gloucester Road
North Yarmouth, ME 04097
(207) 829-5830; fax: (207) 829-6512
Hardy roses, especially old garden and modern shrub roses

Sequoia Nursery/Moore Miniature Roses
2519 East Noble Avenue
Visalia, CA 93292
(209) 732-0190; fax: (209) 732-0192
Miniatures

Stanek's Nursery
2929 East 27th Avenue
Spokane, WA 99223
(509) 535-2939; fax: (509) 534-3050

Thomasville Nurseries
Box 7
Thomasville, GA 31799
(912) 226-5568
Modern roses

Tiny Petals Miniature Roses
489 Minot Avenue
Chula Vista, CA 91910
(619) 422-0385

Trophy Roses, Ltd.
1308 N. Kennicott Avenue
Arlington Heights, IL 60004
(708) 253-0998
Exhibition and custom budded roses

U.S. Measure and Metric Measure Conversion Chart

		Formulas for Exact Measures			Rounded Measures for Quick Reference		
	Symbol	When you know:	Multiply by:	To find:			
Mass (weight)	oz	ounces	28.35	grams	1 oz		= 30 g
	lb	pounds	0.45	kilograms	4 oz		= 115 g
	g	grams	0.035	ounces	8 oz		= 225 g
	kg	kilograms	2.2	pounds	16 oz	= 1 lb	= 450 g
					32 oz	= 2 lb	= 900 g
					36 oz	= 2¼ lb	= 1000 g (1 kg)
Volume	pt	pints	0.47	liters	1 c	= 8 oz	= 250 ml
	qt	quarts	0.95	liters	2 c (1 pt)	= 16 oz	= 500 ml
	gal	gallons	3.785	liters	4 c (1 qt)	= 32 oz	= 1 liter
	ml	milliliters	0.034	fluid ounces	4 qt (1 gal)	= 128 oz	= 3¾ liter
Length	in.	inches	2.54	centimeters	⅜ in.	= 1.0 cm	
	ft	feet	30.48	centimeters	1 in.	= 2.5 cm	
	yd	yards	0.9144	meters	2 in.	= 5.0 cm	
	mi	miles	1.609	kilometers	2½ in.	= 6.5 cm	
	km	kilometers	0.621	miles	12 in. (1 ft)	= 30 cm	
	m	meters	1.094	yards	1 yd	= 90 cm	
	cm	centimeters	0.39	inches	100 ft	= 30 m	
					1 mi	= 1.6 km	
Temperature	° F	Fahrenheit	⅝ (after subtracting 32)	Celsius	32° F	= 0° C	
	° C	Celsius	⅑ (then add 32)	Fahrenheit	212° F	= 100° C	
Area	in.^{2}	square inches	6.452	square centimeters	1 in.^{2}	= 6.5 cm^2	
	ft^2	square feet	929.0	square centimeters	1 ft^2	= 930 cm^2	
	yd^2	square yards	8361.0	square centimeters	1 yd^2	= 8360 cm^2	
	a.	acres	0.4047	hectares	1 a.	= 4050 m^2	